Breaking Into the Big Leagues

*To Roberto —
Sincere Wishes
for the Very Best,
Regards
Al*

Al Goldis
and
Rick Wolff

Leisure Press
Champaign, Illinois

Developmental Editor: Sue Ingels Mauck
Copy Editor: Molly Bentsen
Assistant Editor: JoAnne Cline
Production Director: Ernie Noa
Projects Manager: Lezli Harris
Typesetter: Sandra Meier
Text Design: Keith Blomberg
Text Layout: Gordon Cohen
Cover Design: Conundrum Designs
Cover Photo: Jim Corley
Printed By: Versa Press

Credit is given for photos used from the following sources:

P. 1, Ozzie Guillen, courtesy The Sporting Views, Tony Inzerillo, 291 Andy Dr., Melrose Park, IL © Copyrighted; p. 7, Pete Rose, © Copyright Cincinnati Reds; p. 19, Shawon Dunston, courtesy Chicago Cubs; p. 31, Harold Baines, courtesy The Sporting Views, Tony Inzerillo, 291 Andy Dr., Melrose Park, IL © Copyrighted; p. 41, B.J. Surhoff, courtesy Milwaukee Brewers; p. 65, Bill Swift, courtesy *Bangor Daily News;* p. 79, Comiskey Park, courtesy Jim Corley; p. 95, Vince Coleman, Spectra-Action, Inc., St. Louis, MO; p. 107, Craig Shipley, © Copyright 1985 Los Angeles Dodgers, Inc.

ISBN: 0-88011-298-0

Library of Congress Cataloging-in-Publication Data

Goldis, Al, 1942–
    Breaking into the big leagues.

    Includes index.
    1. Baseball. I. Wolff, Rick, 1951–
II. Title.
GV867.3.G64   1988   796.357   87-15320
ISBN 0-88011-298-0

Printed in the United States of America

10 9 8 7 6 5 4 3 2

Leisure Press
A division of Human Kinetics Publishers, Inc.
Box 5076, Champaign, IL 61825-5076
1-800-747-4457

UK Office:
Human Kinetics Publishers (UK) Ltd.
P.O. Box 18
Rawdon, Leeds LS19 6TG
England
(0532) 504211

Dedication

I would like to dedicate this book to the memory of my late wife, Marlene Goldis, to my parents, Dorothy and the late Samuel Goldis, and to my present wife, Linda Goldis. Their support, encouragement, and commitment have been a source of inspiration and motivation for my baseball coaching and scouting careers.

Acknowledgments

As is true with most books, the people who worked behind the scenes on *Breaking Into the Big Leagues* contributed just as much to the development of the book as the two of us did. To all of them, we offer a hearty "high-five" and a heartfelt thank you for their diverse efforts.

Other thanks are due, too:

To our respective families, especially our wives Linda and Patricia, for putting up with the hours away from them that this project required.

To Dorothy and Samuel Goldis, who inspired Al and gave of their lives so he could play a kids' game that he loves so much.

To Larry Himes, the former scouting director of the California Angels and current general manager of the Chicago White Sox, who gave Al the responsibility, authority, and direction to grow as a scout and administrator.

To our partners in publishing, Brian and Georgene Zevnik of Wellington Press, Inc., who helped massage the manuscript into its final form.

To Jack Moses, Al's first baseball coach, who had the confidence to put an 8-year-old on the same team with 15-year-olds in the Belmont Plateau League in Philadelphia.

To Tony Coma, Al's high school coach, who taught him how to win and the meaning of commitment and dedication.

To "Reds" Sokel and Myron Gilbert, who spent thousands of hours throwing batting practice and "peppering" with Al, from his seventh birthday until he signed with the Cincinnati Reds.

To Ed Liberatore, who signed Al and gave him not only the opportunity to play professional baseball, but also solid direction and leadership.

To John Stokoe and the Baltimore Orioles, who gave Al his first chance to scout in pro ball.

To Joe McIlvaine, who paved the way for Al to become the eastern scouting supervisor for the Angels.

To Nick Kamzic, friend and super scout, who helped Al develop and refine his scouting abilities.

To Jon Scher and Allan Simpson of *Baseball America*, who have forgotten more about baseball than most people will ever know.

To Larry Halstead, president of the *Baseball Blue Book*, who graciously allowed us to crib from his "bible" for our appendix.

To Bill Winslow of the Winslow Research Institute, for his kindness in helping us with the Athletic Motivation Inventory program.

To all the individuals we have quoted or referred to, without whom our subject would lack its excitement and verve.

To baseball's associates throughout the years, for creating and sustaining America's national pastime.

And finally, to you the reader: Every idea needs a spark to set it in motion, and you were it for us. Enjoy!

Contents

Foreword

This is a book that should have been written a long time ago.

You see, it's for every youngster who has ever pulled on a baseball glove or swung a bat and dreamed of some day playing in the major leagues. It's for every maturing young ballplayer who has tried to turn that dream into reality with a mixture of sweat and persistence. It's also for all those young-at-heart baseball fans who are intrigued by what goes on behind the scenes of one of sports' oldest and most revered art forms.

And believe me, scouting a potential professional baseball player is much more of an art than a science. Oh, there are the requisite computer print-outs and Combine statistics and stopwatches and radar guns.

Scouting is a vital and essential part of baseball; indeed, it is where the game has its deepest roots. Scouts have roamed the American country-side since baseball began, hoping to find that million-dollar player in the sawbuck town right around the bend in the road. To many observers, scouts represent the purest dedication to the sport—they do what they do mainly for their love of the game.

No one claims that scouting is easy. That's why this book is so essential. A scout has to evaluate each ballplayer's potential as a major leaguer, not just whether he is an outstanding high school or college player. This is a key distinction, but one that busy scouts rarely have time to explain in detail to a hopeful ballplayer or his parents.

This is precisely why *Breaking Into the Big Leagues* is right on target. Not only do Al Goldis and Rick Wolff explain the process and system of scouting, they carefully detail what scouts are really looking for and why. That's an area that needs clarifying for all baseball fans. Believe me, by the time you've finished this volume you'll know precisely what it takes to be considered a professional prospect. And you'll also read stories from the inside lore of the scouting game.

Sure, scouting is an art, but all artists work from preliminary outlines and sketches. They know what they are looking for before they put the paint to the canvas. The same is true with scouts; they, too, have concrete ideas of what they're looking for when they head out to the ballpark. And it can only help your chances of being spotted and signed if you know the sketches and outlines that scouts today are working from. *Breaking Into the Big Leagues* is the perfect map to use in your quest to become a professional ballplayer.

Larry Himes
General Manager
Chicago White Sox

Preface

This book was written for every ballplayer who has long dreamed of the day he'd be offered a professional baseball contract. But it's not a book for dreamers: It's for realists.

You've probably heard the discouraging statistics from your coaches, your parents, the media, maybe even from your friends. Only one out of thousands of amateur ballplayers gets offered a professional contract. Only 5% of all minor leaguers ever go on to wear major league uniforms.

But the numbers shouldn't deter the young man who dreams of someday making the grade as a professional player. Don't give up when you've worked as hard as you can to develop your talents, when you've done everything your coaches ever asked of you, when you perform well enough to make an all-league or all-star team, but still you get no bites from the pros.

Instead of getting discouraged, ask these two questions: (1) Just what are the scouts looking for in a prospect, and (2) How do I get them to notice me? This book was written to provide answers to those questions and to describe how many major leaguers faced the discouraging statistics and overcame them.

You'll read plenty of case examples of current major leaguers. You'll learn what scouts are looking for and what they write in their reports. You'll get an inside peek at forms and file cards used by top scouts. In fact, by the time you finish this book, you should understand what scouts are most interested in seeing in prospects and how you can make yourself most attractive to them.

We've included many inspirational stories about players who believed in themselves and persevered until they finally got a crack at their dream—and made the most of their opportunities. Some of the names you'll recognize immediately. Others may not be household names—yet. But they all have one thing in common: They are all professional baseball players.

We were two of the lucky, and persistent, ones. We both played baseball in professional organizations—Al with the Cincinnati Reds and Rick with the Detroit Tigers. We both remember the thrill of being offered a professional contract: It was the dream of a lifetime coming true.

In the time since our playing careers ended, we have maintained ties to the national pastime. Al has become one of the game's most respected scouts, and Rick has gained recognition as a college coach, a sportswriter, and a television commentator. But that common thread of being a professional ballplayer still links us—and inspired us to write this book.

When this book was first conceived, Al was the eastern regional supervisor of scouts for the California Angels. However, during the fall of 1986, he was hired by the Chicago White Sox as director of scouting for the entire White Sox organization.

This book represents many hours of collaboration between the two of us, with the goal of filling a need for ballplayers, parents, and coaches. Many of the book's examples are of people and events from Al's experiences with the Angels' organization. All of the first-person references are the accumulation of Al's experiences throughout his scouting career.

If you want to know what the scouts are looking for, and you want to make sure they look at you, then this book is for you. It may not get you signed, but then again. . . .

Al Goldis
Rick Wolff

Chapter 1

Beating the Odds

Every young baseball player wants to be discovered and get a shot at the major leagues. And every professional scout wants to find that "diamond in the rough"—the player everyone else missed but who turns into a superstar. The chances of that player and that scout getting together are slim, but this book will show you how to improve the odds.

Most baseball players and their parents and coaches hear every year about the first-round draft choices, those ballplayers tabbed as "can't-miss" prospects who sign lucrative professional contracts. But one must keep in mind that the players who sign these first-round contracts are rare, and the dollar amounts of their contracts are often grossly exaggerated when reported by the press.

The irony of all these first-round "bonus babies" is that many never pan out. In fact, a breakdown of the first-rounders of the last few years shows that almost half these can't-miss prospects do, in fact, miss: They never develop into major league stars or even regulars.

Our point is that the art of scouting is just that—an art, not a science. There are so many intangibles in judging a player's ability and predicting his physical and mental development that scouting may appear to be little more than an elaborate guessing game.

Yet each year, the June free agent draft comes and goes, and for 700 to 800 ballplayers, the dream of getting the opportunity to play pro baseball comes true. But for the tens of thousands of other players not chosen by a club, there seems to be no recourse but to give up hope. That hope, though, is the first ingredient in pursuing any life dream. Mix it with hard work, determination, talent, and a pinch of good luck, and you may be on your way to signing that professional contract. This book is aimed primarily at the ballplayer who hasn't been drafted but still hopes to play pro ball: You're the individual we're trying to reach.

The purpose of this book is twofold: to give you an inside look at just what scouts are looking for in their search for professional ballplayers and to help you market and sell yourself so that the scouts know you exist and see you put your best skills on display. This book has been written with the intent of helping you keep your dream alive and flourishing. All any ballplayer wants is a shot at playing pro ball. We hope that by the time you finish reading this book, you'll be that much closer to your dream coming true.

"But I Wasn't Drafted . . ."

There are two ways to become a professional ballplayer. The first, and admittedly easier, of the two is to be selected in the June free agent draft that major league teams hold each year. The second is to be signed as an undrafted free agent, that is, a ballplayer who for some reason was bypassed by the draft and is approached and signed to a contract by a particular scout for a particular team.

It makes no difference to the ballclub whether you're drafted or signed as a free agent. Once you get to a minor league club, all you will be judged on is your ability and potential as a professional player. No manager or coach will ask whether you were drafted or signed as an undrafted free agent. They could care less: All they care about is whether you can play.

Sure, there's usually a lot more excitement when your phone rings or a telegram arrives on the day of the draft to inform you that you've been selected by a major league club. But professional baseball is just that—a profession. All you should really care about is getting that shot at pro ball and, ideally, the major leagues. The bottom line is becoming a professional—how you get there really makes little difference.

So if you don't get drafted, shrug it off, keep working at your craft, and forge ahead. If you have the ability and you're clever enough to play in an arena where the scouts can find you, don't worry—they will.

A 1986 article in *Baseball America* revealed that of the 624 current major leaguers, 76 were signed as undrafted free agents.[1] That means that almost one-sixth of all the guys in the big leagues were *not* signed as draft choices!

That's a significant statistic: It should encourage you to pursue your dream of playing major league baseball as far as you want to. You never know when that scout will approach you to ask if you're interested in playing pro ball.

A Big-League All-Star Team That the Scouts Didn't Draft

Perhaps a better way to dramatize this statistic is by giving some examples. As you read the next few pages, put yourself in these players' spikes. Remember that each one suffered from that nagging doubt—not whether he was good enough, but whether he would ever get the chance to play professional baseball.

Catcher: Rich Gedman, Boston Red Sox

Gedman, a local product out of Worcester, Massachusetts, was a pitcher and first baseman in high school. He was passed by in the June draft, but Bosox scout Bill Enos signed Gedman up after seeing him catch while playing American Legion ball.

First base: Andre Thornton, Cleveland Indians

Overlooked entirely in the 1967 draft when he was a senior at Phoenixville (Pennsylvania) High School, Thornton was signed by the Philadelphia Phillies as a free agent while playing amateur ball the summer after he graduated.

---

[1]Scher, J., & Simpson, A. (1986). Baseball's draft system is far from perfect. *Baseball America*, 6(9), 3.

Second base: Frank White, Kansas City Royals

He went to a high school in Kansas City, Missouri, that didn't have a baseball team, but based upon his physical abilities and potential, White was selected at a tryout camp held by the Royals and sent to their now-defunct Baseball Academy. He became the Academy's first graduate to receive a professional contract.

Third base: Ken Oberkfell, Atlanta Braves

Named a junior college all-American after playing just one year at Belleville (Illinois) Junior College, Oberkfell decided to sign with the St. Louis Cardinals prior to the 1975 free agent draft.

Shortstop: Kevin Mitchell, San Francisco Giants

Mitchell, who grew up in a tough neighborhood in San Diego, dropped out of high school. However, he got a break when his cousin, former Mets outfield prospect Darryl Denby, persuaded Mitchell to play with him on a winter league team in San Diego. It was there that the Mets' scouts saw Mitchell play and offered him a contract.

Outfield: Brian Downing, California Angels

Downing played at Cypress (California) Junior College for a year. In the summer of 1969, after he attended a tryout camp with the Chicago White Sox, Downing was offered and signed a contract.

Outfield: Gary Ward, New York Yankees

Totally bypassed in the June free agent draft in 1972 when he graduated from high school in Compton, California, Ward was signed as an undrafted free agent by the Minnesota Twins that summer.

Outfield: Jeffrey Leonard, San Francisco Giants

As a senior at Overbrook High School in Philadelphia, Leonard went undrafted in 1973. But the Los Angeles Dodgers took a chance on Leonard after seeing him play that summer.

Designated hitter: Larry Parrish, Texas Rangers

Parrish had a great career at Florida's Seminole Junior College, but the scouts decided not to draft him. He got a break and was signed by the Montreal Expos as an undrafted player.

Starting pitcher: Rick Mahler, Atlanta Braves

Mahler had a stellar career at tiny Trinity University in San Antonio, Texas, but the scouts weren't interested enough to draft him after his senior year in 1975. The Braves signed him as just another free agent.

Starting pitcher: Bob Ojeda, New York Mets

Ojeda pitched at the College of the Sequoias in Visalia, California, but went undrafted. The Red Sox took a chance on him before the Mets obtained him in a trade in 1985.

Relief pitcher: Jeff Reardon, Minnesota Twins

Reardon was actually drafted out of high school by the Expos, but after he pitched for four years at the University of Massachusetts, the scouts were no longer interested in drafting him. The Mets signed Reardon the summer after he finished college while he was pitching in a semipro league in Canada.

Relief pitcher: Dan Quisenberry, Kansas City Royals

Even though Quisenberry put together a 19-7 record at LaVerne College in LaVerne, California in 1975, the scouts weren't too sure of his under-arm delivery. In fact, they were so uncertain of his style that not one team drafted him. The Royals finally decided to give Quisenberry a shot on one of their low Class A teams and signed him to a contract.

Ironically, in 1985, both Reardon and Quisenberry were named winners of the Rolaids' Fireman of the Year Award, given annually to the best relief pitchers in the majors. Not too bad for two players who signed as free agents.

Are There Others Who Almost Fell Between the Cracks?

There are plenty. Don't forget Claudell Washington—he was never drafted as a prospect but signed with the Oakland As as a free agent. And that's how Bob Brenley ended up with the San Francisco Giants.

Some ballclubs seem to specialize in finding talented ballplayers who are bypassed by the draft. The Phillies, for example, have signed nine undrafted players who eventually made it to the majors. In addition to Andre Thornton, the Chicago Cubs' Bob Dernier was originally found and signed by the Phillies. Others include Philly signees Jeff Stone, Chris James, Rick Schu, and Don Carman.

The list continues:

- The Dodgers found Tom Niedenfuer pitching in the National Baseball Congress' summer semipro tournament in Wichita, Kansas, and signed him as an undrafted free agent.

- Seattle Mariner relief pitcher Mark Huismann grew up in Colorado and pitched at Colorado State. But it wasn't until Huismann was pitching in a semipro league that he caught the attention of the scouts and was signed by the Royals as a free agent.
- Mike Kingery, a hard-hitting outfielder for the Royals, was discovered by Kansas City scouts. Says Art Stewart, scouting director for the Royals, "We found Kingery in an American Legion tournament in August." Why didn't any team draft Kingery out of high school? Offers Stewart, "There was no way we could have drafted him. His high school team in Atwater, Minnesota, played about eight games."
- The Angels found pitcher Kirk McCaskill when he was pitching for the University of Vermont in Burlington, near the Canadian border.

Sometimes scouts spot a talented amateur who appears to be playing out of position. Relief specialist Don Carman, an undrafted player, originally attended a Phillies tryout camp as a first baseman. The Phillies convinced him he had more of a future on the mound.

San Diego Padres outfielder Marvell Wynne changed positions in the other direction. He originally attended a Royals tryout camp as a pitcher. Art Stewart says that Wynne "ran a 60-yard dash and flew like blazes. He said he'd played a little outfield, so we put him out there and he handled himself well." Wynne traded his earned run average for a batting average and was on his way to the majors.

Not all major leaguers were first- or second-round draft choices; many were selected on the lower rounds of the draft. For example, did you know that the New York Yankees' Don Mattingly was a 16th-round draft choice? Or that Ryne Sandberg of the Chicago Cubs was drafted on the 21st round? What about Bill Russell, the long-time Dodgers star? He was taken on the 37th round. And Keith Hernandez of the Mets was chosen on the 42nd round!

By now, the point has been made. Even if you have great talent, you still need inner drive, determination, and psychological and physical stamina to rise through the minors to the big leagues. But as you read through this book, keep in mind the big league names and recall each individual's story of his big break and how he got a scout to take a gamble on him.

If there were only a few of these unusual signing stories, they might be written off as exceptions or flukes. But there are many of these occurrences, and they cannot simply be dismissed: They are more proof that major league scouting is still more art than science.

Chapter 2

The Scouting System

Each of the 26 major league clubs, as well as the Major League Scouting Bureau, has its own hierarchy of scouts. Although I'm most familiar with the California Angels and Chicago White Sox set-ups, many clubs have organized their scouting systems in a similar way.

It is important for you to understand the differences among various scouts. By knowing how a scouting system is set up, you'll have a clearer idea of your chances of getting signed. Here's a look at a typical scouting organization from the bottom up.

Associate Scouts

First is the *associate scout*, affectionately known as a "bird dog." These individuals, who beat the high school, college and semipro bushes in hopes of flushing out potential prospects (hence the bird dog nickname), are affiliated with particular major league clubs, but usually do not receive salaries. Instead they may receive commissions; that is, if a bird dog finds a prospect who does sign with the club, then the front office rewards the scout with a bonus.

These men, rather than making scouting an occupation, just attend ball games whenever they can. If they spot a potential prospect, they get the word back to their scouting superiors. If a scout ever approaches you while you are playing at the high school, American Legion, Babe Ruth, junior college, or sandlot level, he most likely will be a bird dog. He may ask you some questions about your education, your school, your age, and so forth. He may even ask for a schedule of your games and where you expect to be playing that summer.

If an associate scout finds a player he likes, he'll notify the club's part-time or full-time scout in that area. Sometimes the notice will be in writing; other times it will be verbal. The point is, if a bird dog thinks you have some professional promise, he'll get the word back to the next scouting level.

Part-Time and Full-Time Scouts

Again, organizations differ, but by and large, a *part-time scout* draws either a small salary or just travel expenses and has another full-time job, perhaps as a teacher or coach himself. He usually scouts in the area where he lives. If he is tipped off by a bird dog to a prospect, he will most likely check out the player in question. If he likes what he sees, he'll give the prospect an information card like the ones in Figures 2.1 and 2.2 to fill out.

The completed forms usually go to the ballclub's *full-time area scout*. In most cases, he has the authority to recommend that a young man be drafted and signed to a contract. However, as you'll discover, there's a big difference between recommending a player be drafted and signed and actually seeing it happen.

You can be given a prospect card at any age, particularly if you look good in a tryout camp or are an underclassman in high school. It is no guarantee of being signed, but it's definitely a step in the right direction.

Figure 2.1.

Prospect Information Form

Name _____ Phone _____

Address _____

City _____ State _____ Zip _____

Father's Name _____ Occupation _____

Mother's Name _____ Occupation _____

Has anyone in your family played professional baseball? Any close friends?

_____

Has anyone in your family graduated from college? From what school(s)?

_____

What professional baseball organizations have contacted you concerning a baseball career?

_____

Have any colleges or universities offered you a full scholarship or other financial assistance?

_____

What is your grade point average? _____

Are you considering one school more strongly than the others? Have you signed a national letter of intent to attend any of the schools? _____

How many sports do you participate in and what individual honors have you been awarded in each? Also list your batting average, HRs or ERA, and Won-Loss record for the past two seasons.

_____

_____

_____

Figure 2.2.

Information Card

Give this card to all players you have an interest in. You will need information to complete the cross-check alert—use the card to expedite information gathering. You can place your return address and stamp on this card and have the prospect or coach forward to you by mail. If possible, get all information immediately.

- Date
- Name (first, middle, last)
- Address (street, city, state, zip code)
- Telephone (with area code)
- Position
- Date of birth (month, day, year)
- Height
- Weight
- Marital Status
- Glasses or contacts?
- Bat (right, left, switch)
- Throw (right, left)
- High school/college graduation (month, day, year)
- Address of school (street, city, state, zip code, telephone)
- Plan to attend college?
- College preference
- Name of baseball coach (telephone)
- Do you play American Legion baseball? (club name)
- Other amateur club
- Have you ever been drafted by a professional club? (name)
- Parents' names
- Parents' address (street, city, state, zip code, telephone)

An area scout is generally assigned to one region. In densely populated areas, there might be as many as three area scouts. For example, in the New York–New Jersey–Connecticut area, some clubs will have three full-time scouts looking for prospects. Why? Mainly because there are a lot of kids to see in a short period of time. In areas that are less densely populated, such as North and South Dakota or Vermont and New Hampshire, there might be just one full-time or even part-time scout.

A Typical Case

Let's assume that you're a pretty good player and that you've been playing ball in school all spring. Now you're getting ready for the summer leagues. A bird dog in your town has read about your accomplishments in the local paper and has had a chance to see you play. He liked what he saw, and he got the word back to the part-time scout.

The part-time scout came to see you play the following weekend. He liked your speed and actions, so he alerted the area scout. The area scout looked over his schedule of high school and summer league games and realized that he could see you play on a particular Saturday when your team would play a crosstown rival. He had heard about a possible prospect on the other team as well and figured he could watch you play against each other.

On that Saturday, you showed your stuff so well that the scout came down to introduce himself after the game. He asked a few questions and gave you a prospect card to fill out. He also told you about a tryout camp later that summer and said he'd like you to attend.

Where Do I Sign?

At this point, you're ready to jump up in the air, pop the corks on the champagne, and tell your family and friends that you're going to be a major leaguer. But even though you've made it to the area scout's follow-up list, there's certainly no guarantee that you're going to be drafted and signed, much less make it to the big leagues.

Certainly being approached by a scout is some cause for celebration. After all, if the associate scout didn't like what he saw, he would not have told the part-time scout about you. And if the part-time scout didn't like what he saw, he wouldn't have recommended you to the full-time scout. And the area scout has taken a liking to you. But that only means that he'll want to follow your progress. If, after watching you a few more times, he still thinks you're a prospect, only then will he recommend that the *regional scouting supervisor* see you play for the possibility of being drafted.

By this point you would have gone through an extensive filtering process that is the essence of scouting. You've been scouted numerous times by the associate, the part-time, and now the full-time area scouts, who agree that you possess some professional tools. But next you have to impress the regional scouting supervisor.

On occasion, an area scout can sign a ballplayer without the approval of the regional scouting supervisor. This usually occurs just after the June free agent draft, when the club's front office realizes that it doesn't have enough catchers, shortstops, left-handed pitchers, or whatever, to fill out their Class A or Rookie League team. When that kind of shortage occurs, the word goes out to the various area scouts to be on the lookout for any youngster who plays the needed position but was bypassed in the draft.

The area scouts then go over their lists of kids who were impressive, but for some reason were not drafted. If a scout has a youngster he thinks is suitable, he notifies the front office. The front office normally gives its permission for the scout to sign the prospect and even give him a token bonus of perhaps $500 or $1000. The youngster who gets signed by this route is usually a rugged, determined young man who makes the very most of his opportunity to play pro ball.

Players like Pete Rose got the chance to play ball in this fashion. Paul Snyder, director of scouting for the Atlanta Braves, admits that back in 1960 when Rose first signed with the Cincinnati Reds for $500, he was a real gamble from a scouting point of view. Says Snyder, "If you graded Pete Rose out, all his tools would have been below average, except for [hitting] contact."

Most scouts agree with that assessment. Rose has never been considered a hitter with great power, or a base runner with outstanding speed, or a terrific fielder, or a player with a great gun for an arm. But Pete always could hit, and he did have that classic Hall-of-Fame determination and desire, characteristics that are difficult to gauge. "You can't cut someone open and see what's inside," continues Snyder. "You can't measure their intestinal fortitude."

The Regional Scouting Supervisor's Analysis

If an area scout likes you as a prospect, he'll recommend you as a possible draft selection for his major league club. At this point, sometime before the June draft, the regional scouting supervisor will come to see you play as well. This scout oversees the various area scouts in one section of the country, and he has the perspective to judge and compare ballplayers throughout his assigned region.

A Definite "First-Rounder"

Let's take our fantasy—your fantasy—one step farther. Suppose the regional scouting supervisor thinks you're a dynamite prospect, too. In his reports, he pushes you as a top draft choice, possibly even a first-round pick. You may even get an impressive final draft recommendation like the one in Figure 2.3 (see chapter 4 for an explanation of the numbers used).

Once the front office learns this, the big boss—the *scouting director*—would dispatch his national cross-checker to look you over. In this highly selective system, the cross-checker is one more way of making certain that the other scouts who have seen you haven't missed something. The national cross-checker sees the best prospects from every region in the country, so when he sees you, he can compare you with the best prospects from the East, the West, the Midwest, and so on.

The cross-checker's report will focus on your draft ranking. For example, he may think that you're definitely the best prospect in your region, but out of four national regions, you only rate fourth. Sometimes the best position player in one region may not be as good a prospect as even the fifth-ranked prospect in another. Or one region may have the best prospects in every position or the best in a specific position category.

Continuing our story—the national cross-checker has seen you play, and he reports to the scouting director that, in his opinion, you are not only a top prospect, you're the best prospect in the country. With this kind of recommendation, you can be sure that the club's scouting director will come to see you play. He will want to see for himself just how good you are before putting your name at the top of the club's list of prospects. If you're the top national pick, chances are you will get a financial bonus. Before he tells the club owner that he plans to sign you and give you that bonus, the scouting director obviously wants to see what his money is going to buy.

A Simplistic Overview

As you can imagine, the scenario above was simplified in many ways, but you get the main idea. Each ballclub's scouting system is based on an intricate network of checks and double-checks. By the time a club has projected you as a top pick, up to four scouts from that club alone have seen you play many times.

But even after you have gained the approval of these experienced scouts, there is no promise of success in the major leagues. Out of a typical first

Figure 2.3.

Draft Recommendation

Type prospect: __Above average__
Grade: __54__

Name: _____
Address: _____
Team name: _____

Height: __6'0"__   Weight: _190_   Age: __18__   Grade: _Sr_
Bats: _R_   Throws: _R_   Position: _RF_

Preference Pick: __8th Round__

Position player   **Pitcher**
   Hit __30/50__   Fastball _____
   Power __50/60__   Curve _____
   Speed __60/60__   Slider _____
   Arm __40/40__   Change _____
   Field __40/60__   Other pitch _____
   Base running __40/60__   Control _____
   Bat speed __60__   Arm action _____
   Contact __40__   Delivery _____
   Make-up _50_   Make-up _____

Type hitter: _Line drive, average power_

Medical problems: _Sprained right ankle last year while playing basketball—OK now._

Signability: _Has scholarship offers at two top colleges (_____ and _____) and the GPA to choose either, but he wants to be a ML ballplayer. Has cousin who plays in minors and uncle who formerly played with several organizations. Mother is very education-oriented. Scholarship program could be plus that convinces him to sign._

Other remarks: _Good all-around athlete. Lots of class. I recommend $ _____ range to sign._

round of 26 players selected—that is, the first-round draftees—only about 40% ever stick on a major league roster. That means that more than half of the players picked on the first round never make it for any length of time in the big leagues. Thus, you can see that even the best scouting system is fallible and that the so-called can't-miss player is almost never found.

There is a positive side to this coin, too. Here is an example: In the June 1986 draft, pitcher Greg Swindell of the University of Texas was considered one of nation's best prospects. Lefty Swindell had all the tools to become a bona fide major leaguer, and the top scouts' consensus was that this youngster was for real. The irony of the situation is that when Swindell was in high school, not only was he not drafted by any team, he wasn't even the number-one pitcher on his high school team!

Just three years earlier, as a senior at Sharpstown High in Houston, Swindell threw strikes, but only at 82 mph. With a few years of maturation and arm strengthening, Swindell retained his control and boosted his velocity to 93 mph. Not even the best scouts foresaw that.

Roger Clemens, another pitcher from the Houston area, threw only in the low 80s when he was in high school. But because he was a good-sized kid (6'-3'', 210 pounds), the Twins drafted Clemens in the 22nd round out of high school and hoped he'd sign.

Clemens, torn between playing pro ball and going to college at the University of Texas, finally decided to attend San Jacinto Junior College before playing ball for Cliff Gustafson in Austin. For Clemens, it was the right decision. Three years later, he led the Longhorns to the 1983 NCAA College World Series title, having added another 10 mph to his fastball. Clemens was a first-round pick for the Bosox that year and the American League Cy Young award winner in 1986.

The Major League Scouting Bureau

In the early 1960s, baseball club owners began to realize that some organizations, such as the New York Yankees and Los Angeles Dodgers, had become particularly efficient at signing prospects and then keeping them employed on farm teams. Scouts tried to hide any prospects they found, in hopes of signing the best players for their own system. In those days, scouts would "babysit" their prospects and shoo away any other scouts, so they wouldn't have to get involved in bidding contests for players.

Baseball owners soon realized that a system was developing in which the better, and wealthier, teams were establishing dynasties of talent. The teams with less talent and less money just couldn't compete, either on the field or in the pocketbook pursuit of prospects. It was a case of the rich becoming richer. To insert a sense of parity into the game, the free agent draft system as we know it today was instituted in 1965.

The concept of the annual free agent draft was to allow the major league club with the worst record from the previous season to select first in the draft of all eligible prospects. Then the team with the second-worst record selected, and so on. In this manner, the owners were attempting to return a sense of equality to the game, so that no club had an advantage in scouting and signing free agent prospects. It was an effort to help the poor become richer.

Many scouts felt that their talents were shortchanged as a result of the June free agent draft. Most scouts enjoyed the challenge of finding, secluding, and eventually signing prospects that their counterparts had missed. But with the free agent draft system in place, the scouts felt that it no longer mattered whether they found a hot prospect first or last. After all, if another ballclub selected ahead of the scout's in the next draft, then the other club could tap that prospect—and the scout who originally found the player could do nothing about it.

The free agent draft, for the most part, has worked extremely well in accomplishing its original purpose. Another result has been the establishment of the Major League Scouting Bureau (MLSB). The ballclub owners, realizing that talented prospects would be signed not according to the scouts who found the players but rather by each team's place in the selection process, decided to hire a network of scouts to comb the countryside for prospects. These MLSB scouts would evaluate youngsters just like other scouts did, but instead of filing a report with an individual ballclub, they would file their reports with the MLSB.

According to Jim Fanning, now of the Montreal Expos, the purpose of the Bureau was merely to supplement each ballclub's own scouting system, not to replace it. Unfortunately, during the 1970s, as some teams began to cut back on their operating expenses, many scouts were lopped off the payroll, and more and more emphasis was placed on the reports filed by MLSB scouts.

This movement tended to defeat the purpose of the MLSB and weakened many teams in the process. In their efforts to cut costs, some owners had forgotten the MLSB's original purpose—to supplement, not to replace. "The original intent was not to get the clubs to reduce their number of scouts," says Fanning. "It was to be an aid in the field. What has happened is that many clubs have reduced their number of scouts and have relied almost entirely on the Scouting Bureau."

Every front office in baseball has its own philosophy of what the club needs to become the world champion. Some clubs think the key is team speed. Others emphasize pitching. Still others think that a solid defense is the answer. And some clubs actually break down their requirements for winning according to position.

If a ballclub wants to emphasize a particular philosophy, then it makes a concerted effort to educate its own scouts as to what it wants. But if a front office is relying strictly on the reports of the centralized Scouting Bureau, it really is flying blind. A ballclub has no way to follow up or to cross-check certain players. During the 1970s, some clubs did rely solely upon the Scouting Bureau for reports. That pattern, fortunately, is changing.

The MLSB currently employs 65 full-time scouts around the country. According to a recent major league decision, all ballclubs now utilize its services in terms of finding players and filing reports. But most, if not all, ballclubs also have their own paid scouts, and the services of the MLSB are now more closely aligned to its original concept.

Most baseball executives and even scouts agree that the MLSB is a terrific idea and that it does work. An example of the system's success is found in Jack Howell, an excellent infielder for the Angels. Jack played college ball at the University of Arizona, a school nationally known for its talent that is well scouted each spring. Despite all the scouts who followed Arizona baseball, Howell was not drafted. After the draft, one of the Angels' scouts saw Howell play again and liked him. Just to double-check, the Angels went back to the MLSB's report on Howell. Sure enough, the Scouting Bureau had pinpointed Howell as one of the top 500 prospects in the country that year. On that basis, the Angels signed him. The result? Within three years of signing, Howell made the big leagues.

Chapter 3

Beating the Bushes for Ballplayers: How Scouts Find Talent

For the professional baseball scout, finding a "diamond in the rough"—
the kid that everybody else missed who turns into a superstar—would be
a dream come true. Scouting stories of how players such as Rod Carew,
Ron LeFlore, and Kirk McCaskill were found and signed to pro contracts
make for fascinating conversation around the batting cage or in the press
box.

- Rod Carew, one of baseball's all-time best hitters, was "discovered"
  and signed by Herb Stein of the Minnesota Twins literally in the
  shadows of Yankee Stadium. Carew, who grew up in the Bronx, used
  to play sandlot ball in Macombs Dam Park, right next to "the house
  that Ruth built." Stein watched Carew, liked what he saw, and signed
  him—a real gem found right in the Yankees' backyard.
- Ron LeFlore was serving time in a Michigan prison when he started
  to play ball for recreation on the prison team. His abilities caught
  the eye of the warden, who got word to Billy Martin, then the manager
  of the Detroit Tigers. Billy actually went to see Ron play inside the
  prison walls. He liked LeFlore's speed, power, and desire, and after
  going through the necessary authorities, signed LeFlore to a contract.
  Ron went on to play and star for several years with the Tigers and
  White Sox.
- I got hot when I found Kirk McCaskill, but it took a trip to one of
  the coldest parts of the country to do it. McCaskill was an all-American
  ice hockey player at the University of Vermont, and he really wanted
  to play pro hockey more than baseball. But after a brief fling in the
  National Hockey League, Kirk realized that he had a better shot of
  making it in sports as a major league pitcher. With that in mind, he
  signed with the Angels and is now a solid starting pitcher for them.

These scouting tales, however, are very much exceptions to the rule.
For every Rod Carew or Ron LeFlore or Kirk McCaskill who's "discovered," there are hundreds of other prospects who are scouted in more con-
ventional fashion. That's an important point, and one you should keep
in mind as you read this chapter. Most scouts are very meticulous in
"mining their territory" in search of that "diamond in the rough."

Will the Scouts Come Out?

Most amateur ballplayers aspiring to the pros assume that at some point
during the season, a number of scouts will come to their games, watch
them, and, if impressed, come back later in the season to observe again.

Is that assumption true? Remember that in any one region of the country, there are only a handful of scouts to look for, locate, and then actually watch young prospects in action. For example, in the New York metropolitan area alone, there are over 500 high schools and more than 100 colleges and junior colleges with varsity baseball programs. All these schools and colleges play their entire schedules in a period of less than three months.

Since the New York area is fertile ground for baseball talent, for three months during the spring, a New York scout runs from one game to another, all week and weekend long. To make matters worse, most schools play their games at the same time, usually 3:00 or 4:00 p.m.

A scout can physically attend only so many games during the course of one afternoon or even one week. As a result, even the most dedicated scout misses a lot more games than he makes during the course of a season. Even if he does make it to one of your games, he might stay for only a few innings before leaving to watch another.

Well, you ask, how about the summer leagues, such as Babe Ruth, American Legion, Stan Musial, Connie Mack, and the rest? Can't scouts watch those games, too? Yes, of course, and they do. But again, there are hundreds of summer leagues, thousands of summer league teams, and tens of thousands of summer league players—and only a handful of scouts in any one region.

Setting Up a Network of Contacts

No matter how hard they try, scouts can't watch ballgames as closely or ballplayers as often as they would like. So what do the better scouts do to insure that they don't miss a diamond in the rough?

Many scouts tackle this problem by setting up a network of reliable contacts. At the start of practice in early spring, a scout may send a "personalized" form letter to the head baseball coach at each high school, college, and junior college in their area.

In this letter, like the one in Figure 3.1, which usually carries the letterhead of the particular baseball club a scout represents, he asks for the coach's assistance in listing the best professional prospects he's seen, either on his own team or a competing one.

There are spaces to list players' names, positions, ages, heights, weights, and so on. The scout also usually requests a team schedule and roster. The letter is generally sent with a self-addressed stamped envelope to make the return as easy as possible.

Figure 3.1.

Coach Information Request

(Scout's name and address)

Dear (Coach):

Would you please forward me a copy of your schedule and roster for the coming year? The baseball season will be getting started soon, and the information I have requested will be very helpful in preparing my scouting activities.

Also, I would appreciate your recommendations of any youngsters you feel the _____ should scout for the coming season. The recommendations could be for players on your team or players you have seen on other clubs.

Recommendations

Name	Position	School	Age	Wt.	Ht.	Remarks

Coach's name:

(Scout's signature)

This system, basically direct mail to coaches, is an effective way to lay a foundation for an information pipeline from the coaches that pinpoints the best players in an area. A coach usually is flattered that a major league scout knows about his school and his program and has written asking for his advice and help. In fact, many coaches post a copy of the scout's letter on the team's bulletin board for all to see. Posting the letter serves as a great motivator for the coach and team because everyone knows the scouts may be watching them.

This method of gathering information becomes particularly effective over a number of years, as the scout develops a feel for each coach and the strength of his recommendations. For example, some coaches write back every year with six or seven can't-miss prospects, all from his team, who turn out to have been overstated. On the other hand are coaches who recommend only one or two prospects each season, often from other teams. The scout, having learned how tough a critic a certain coach is, will take that coach's recommendations very seriously and make certain he sees those kids. That kind of coach gives any aspiring player on his team a big advantage in the race to the majors.

I've found this direct-mail letter approach one of the best ways to learn of prospects. For example, Jimmy Key, who now pitches for the Toronto Blue Jays, first came to my attention when Bill Wilhelm, the head coach at Clemson, listed him on one of these letters. Jimmy wasn't very well known at the time, but after his coach got the word out, he was well scouted and became a high draft choice.

I don't want you to think that scouts listen only to high school or college coaches. I vividly recall a phone call a few years ago from Mel Zitter, a coach of various sandlot teams in Brooklyn. He was calling to tell me about a skinny ninth-grader whom he described as "the best shortstop I've ever seen." Knowing Mel's long-standing reputation as a respected coach of younger players, I had to take some time to go down and see this young phenomenon who hadn't yet played his first game of high school baseball. So, down at the beat-up Parade Grounds in Brooklyn—a field with more rocks than grass—I got my first glimpse of a shy youngster named Shawon Dunston. The kid was nervous and a bit tentative, but it was obvious he had great potential: In fact, four years later, he was the number-one pick in the country, and he is now playing shortstop for the Chicago Cubs.

Newspaper Articles

Kids often poke fun at a teammate who makes a big deal about getting his name in the local paper. But certainly everybody enjoys seeing his name in print, particularly when it reflects a success on the ball field.

From a scout's vantage point, reading local papers to see who's doing well is a major aid in finding and tracking down prospects. If a local paper does a reasonably good job of covering high school and college sports, as most local papers do, then a scout can arrive home after a long day on the road and pick up the paper to see who's doing well elsewhere.

I read all the local papers I can, and I make sure all my area scouts and bird dogs read the sports pages as well. For example, I might read that Jones has pitched his third shutout in as many weeks or that Smith hit two homers in a game. I make mental or written notes to follow up on Jones and Smith later in the season.

Such information is vital for scouts. Suppose, for example, that the hypothetical Jones plays for North Central High School, and that a few weeks ago, when the scout saw North Central play, Jones didn't pitch. After reading the newspaper accounts, the scout knows he has to get back to North Central on a day when Jones is pitching.

Imagine a similar situation for Smith, the heavy hitter. Maybe when the scout saw Smith's high school team play, Smith didn't play well because he was sick or hurt. Now that the scout has read that Smith is hitting the long ball, he may think it's time to go back and see him again.

Naturally, you can't control whether local sportswriters mention you as a good player, but if you have received some coverage in the press, it's a good idea to keep these clippings in a well-organized and neat fashion. If you ever write to a major league scout about your abilities, actual newspaper articles will help to substantiate your claims.

Local Sportswriters

Local sportswriters have an important role in notifying scouts about players' abilities. If your name keeps popping up in game stories or a special feature column, the scouts will be reading about you.

A local writer is assigned to cover most high school and college games. Of course, it would be unwise for you or your parents to call up the sportswriter to brag about what a great prospect you are. But there's nothing wrong with your being friendly with the sportswriter, or, if you're in college, with your school's sports information director. It would be a mistake to ask a writer or publicist directly to write about you, but the better you are known to them, the greater the chance that they will mention you. So cultivate these contacts.

Tournament Play

Particularly during the summer, baseball scouts focus their efforts on tournaments and regional play-off games, for they know that the guys who are serious about baseball and who want to compete against the best are likely to be there.

Thus, if you plan to play on a summer league team, make certain before you sign up that it has a good shot at being invited to play in a tournament at the end of the season or at making the play-offs. Scouts who attend those games can see how you perform both under tournament pressure and against solid competition.

Word-of-Mouth

As comprehensive and systematic as scouts like to think they are in finding their prospects, they hear about players through the proverbial grapevine just like everybody else.

A scout may think he's covered an entire area of the country, then gets a call from someone saying that he's "just seen the greatest ballplayer of all time." Although usually these grapevine prospects have been exaggerated, every so often one produces a real gem.

When I first heard about Bo Jackson, he was a high school student in Alabama. Vince Capece, the Angels' regional scout in the South, had learned about this big, strong, fast kid through the community grapevine. Vince followed up on this word-of-mouth prospect, who turned out to have some merit. Not all leads end with a Bo Jackson, but the occasional success makes the follow-up worthwhile.

Coaches

Most coaches like to be in contact with scouts. They like to be considered as experts and enjoy tipping off a scout about a prospect or two. Whether the baseball being played is college, junior college, high school, American Legion, Babe Ruth, sandlot, or semipro, sharp scouts listen to coaches.

A talented youngster may for some reason attend a school that doesn't have a baseball team, and he does all his playing in the summer leagues. That kind of prospect might slip by a scout, unless the summer league coach contacts him.

Scouts and coaches invariably cross paths. Whether at a ball game or during the off-season at a banquet, baseball convention, or other function, scouts and coaches know each other and are constantly talking about players and prospects.

There's nothing wrong with asking your coach if he would recommend you to a scout. He probably would be willing if he believes that you are a prospect and are interested in a pro career.

Or if you feel that for some reason your own coach is not making sufficient effort to push you and your abilities, there's nothing wrong with going to the coach of another team, especially one you've played well against, and asking for his help. This demands a bit of tact and diplomacy, but other coaches are usually glad to help you out if they think you're a prospect.

A young man named Brian Harvey is currently the hardest-throwing pitcher in the Angels' organization. But when Brian played high school ball in North Carolina, his coach didn't get the word out to the scouts about him. However, his summer league coach was impressed with him and contacted the Angels' regional scout, Alex Cosmidis, who saw Brian throw and signed him on the spot.

Umpires

Many scouts make it a point to get to know the local umpires. Why? Because umps often have the most objective view on ballplayers. They are on the field, right next to the players, or behind home plate. They're right on top of the action, with the best view in the ballpark of just how much that pitcher's curve is breaking, how fast a base stealer is, or what kind of hands the shortstop really has.

Umpires usually work several ball games and see a number of teams during a week. This affords them the opportunity to see ballplayers from a variety of schools and colleges. An ump with a sharp eye thus can be a source of some fairly accurate and objective comparisons.

Umpires also can often provide more than just an analysis of hitting or throwing skills. Since they are right in the heat of the action, they can gain valuable insights into how individual players react under pressure and adversity. They see, for example, how a young and talented pitcher reacts if a teammate makes an error behind him, or if he thinks the home plate ump has missed a call. Umpires can get a better feel for a ballplayer's psychological makeup when a call in the field, such as an attempted second-base steal, goes against him.

Knowing how a player reacts to adversity is a major key in a scout's report to the front office. Does that player shrug off the call, or make a big deal out of it? Does he frequently complain to the ump during a game or go about his actions on the field in a businesslike manner? Does he seem to enjoy himself on the diamond, or to be working under undue pressure?

To the scout looking to sign a prospect, the ballplayer's psychological profile is just as important as his physical abilities (see chapter 5). The scout who takes the time to build up a network of contacts with umpires can gain a few more insights into a ballplayer's abilities.

If you've become friendly with an umpire, there's nothing wrong in telling him about your aspirations. If he feels you have some professional ability, he may give you the name and telephone number of some local scouts; he might even call them himself about you. Most umpires are former ballplayers themselves and would love to help a youngster get signed, especially one who asked for their help.

If you should get the opportunity to call a scout, introduce yourself as a ballplayer; say that you are calling at the suggestion of an umpire and give his name. Tell the scout about your professional aspirations, and let him take it from there. He will probably ask basic information about you and then talk to the umpire. Just call the scout once unless he asks you to call again. Give him time to do his homework on you. It is important, too, that information like the scout's name and number be volunteered by the umpire. If he thinks he can help you, when you ask, he most likely will. If he can't, he probably will tell you so.

Joel Lieber is a highly regarded umpire who works college and semi-pro games in the New York area. A few summers ago, I bumped into Joel when he was officiating a game in the Atlantic Collegiate Baseball League, a well-known summer college league on the East Coast.

While we were chatting, Joel said, "Listen, Al, there's a young right-handed pitcher you ought to see in this league. His name is Phil Venturino—he's a junior out of St. Francis College in Brooklyn."

I had to confess that I hadn't heard much about the kid. Joel pressed on: "He's got an excellent fastball and a hard slider. He's the best I've seen this year in this league."

Then Ralph DiLullo, one of the best-known scouts in the MLSB, told me the same thing. That was convincing enough for me. If Joel and Ralph both liked Venturino, I knew that he was worth following.

Venturino hadn't attracted much attention during his college career due to various injuries and limited playing time. But when I saw him, I knew we had a prospect. After Venturino pitched a few times that summer, the Angels signed him. In his first year of pro ball, he chalked up an impressive 8-3 record, with a 1.97 ERA, in the Midwest League. Those are very good numbers in any league—and it was an umpire who tipped off the Angels to this prospect.

Tryout Camps

Ballplayers do occasionally, though not often, get signed out of tryout camps. And surprisingly, many of these go on to become major leaguers.

Art Howe, who was an excellent hitter for many years with the Pittsburgh Pirates, Houston Astros and several other big league clubs, was signed out of a tryout camp. Howe had been a big football and baseball star at the University of Wyoming, but due to the cold weather of most Wyoming springs, not many scouts saw him play. Upon graduation, he returned to his home in Pittsburgh to work as a computer programmer and played semipro ball for fun. He played so well that his buddies encouraged him to go to a Pirates' tryout camp. He did, he impressed, and he was signed.

Golden Glove infielder Doug Flynn has played with the Reds, Mets, Expos, and Tigers. Like Art Howe, he was encouraged by his friends and teammates to go to a tryout camp. It was at a Reds' camp that Doug got his chance and was signed.

Glenn Meyers is another example I'm familiar with first-hand. As a senior at Columbia University in New York, Glenn hit 22 home runs and was named to the NCAA Academic All-American team. The slugging outfielder was well known to scouts throughout the East, but he was just too slow. You can't sign ballplayers these days if they don't run well. After his great senior year, Meyers waited for the June draft and hoped for the telephone to ring. But the draft came and went, and he began to think that maybe his dream of playing pro ball was just a dream and nothing more.

I didn't know much about Glenn, but I got reports that he was playing semipro ball in a summer league and was continuing his slugging ways. Finally a friend of his called and pleaded with me to look him over one last time. I was conducting a tryout session for a couple of youngsters whom I considered "real" prospects, so I invited Meyers along just to see what he could do—almost as a measuring stick for the other kids.

At the tryout, the first thing I had the kids do was a 60-yard dash. I matched Meyers against another outfielder who was a known speedster, having stolen more than 60 bases during the college season. When the dash was over, Meyers had won by four or five yards, in 6.78 seconds. That's very impressive—especially for a guy who "can't run." Still a bit skeptical, we had Glenn run again. And again. Each dash showed the same kind of results—6.7 and 6.8 seconds for 60 yards.

Suddenly, Glenn Meyers moved from the "no-prospect" category to being considered a real find. We already knew from the scouting reports that he could hit with power and had a good arm. Now, with the discovery that he could run, too, we knew we wanted him. By the next morning Glenn Meyers had signed a pro pact with the Angels, packed his bags, and was on his way to his first professional game.

What was the mystery about his running speed? A little investigation turned up a simple answer. A right-handed batter, Glenn took a ferocious cut at the ball. By the time he untangled himself at the plate, he lost valuable time going down the first-base line. With a few pointers on how to correct that problem, Glenn was on his way. He's a prime example of a ballplayer known by all the scouts who almost fell through the cracks.

How can you excel at a tryout camp? The trick is to be at the peak of your game—a little sharper, a little more polished, and a little bit better prepared than your competition. The players invited to the tryout are presumably among the best in the area; however, only a handful will ever be signed. Your best bet is to have an inside edge. To that end, chapter 7 will give you an in-depth look at what you can expect at a tryout camp and what scouts are looking for in players there.

Chapter 4

How Scouts
Rate Prospects

For every ballplayer who sweats, toils, produces, even prays, for a shot at pro ball, there are many others who never see their lifelong dream fulfilled.

Some, as they continue to play, begin to realize why the scouts pass them by. Gradually they see that they just don't run well enough, or hit the ball consistently, or throw strikes with the kind of velocity that a pro pitcher needs. For such individuals, the passage of time plus the natural maturation process quietly convinces them that they are not quite good enough to get to the big leagues. However, it's the rare individual who comes to this kind of realization in his late teens or early 20s.

Much more common are players with complaints like these:

"I just don't understand it. I hit .440 this past spring, but the scouts signed that other guy, and he hit only .230!"

"They [the scouts] claim I just don't throw hard enough, but look at my stats! Why, I was all-league and all-conference this year, and even threw a no-hitter!"

"One scout was interested, but when he heard I was 24, he said I was too old to sign."

"Okay, I'll admit I'm not much of a fielder, but nobody can hit like I do, and what about that old baseball saying, 'As long as you can hit, you can play'? Well, give me a chance; after all, I can be a DH, can't I?"

Players like these, who may be talented at the high school or college level, may seem to have legitimate gripes. How *is* it possible for a pro scout to pass on a player who has hit .440 and pursue one who finished the college season at .230?

In some ways, scouts have to act as soothsayers. Every scout makes two distinct evaluations of a player. The first is how good a player is today. The second, and much more critical, evaluation is how good this player will be tomorrow. That evaluation, based almost solely on the scout's "educated experience," is the cornerstone of finding professional baseball talent.

Let's use the example of the .440 hitter versus the .230 hitter to illustrate. There is no question that, all other factors being equal, the .440 hitter seems to be the better player. So, in the first evaluation, the better prospect would be the guy who hit over .400.

But with his experienced eye, the scout may realize that the .440 hitter has reached his peak as a player, whereas the fellow who's hitting .230 is just scratching the surface of his athletic potential. The scout predicts that the current .440 hitter will never again come close to the great season he's enjoying this year. He's at the peak of his athletic performance, and his abilities will begin to slide rather than expand.

On the other hand, the scout might foresee big happenings for the youngster who is hitting only .230. Maybe the young man is just developing his strength. Maybe his timing is coming around at the plate. Or maybe he's beginning to put on some needed muscle in his arms and shoulders. Whatever the reason, the scout predicts a bright career for this player as he begins to tap his athletic potential. Based on that prediction—that second evaluation—the scout might offer that .230 hitter a contract.

Rolando Roomes is an example of just such a player. Rolando, from Far Rockaway, New York, was signed as an outfielder strictly because of his tremendous power. A big kid, Roomes struck out an awful lot in high school and was never considered the most consistent player in the area. But every so often he would give the ball a good, long ride. Based upon that home run power and future potential, Roomes was signed by Billy Blitzer of the Chicago Cubs.

Was this fair? After all, the basic rule of competitive sports is that if you work hard and produce, someday you'll be rewarded for your victories and accomplishments. And every scout would agree that the player who hit .440 is entitled to every award, honor, citation, and recognition that he can get. The scouts will point to his final statistics and say, "Look—this guy hit .440. He had a helluva year!"

But just because a ballplayer has a great year doesn't mean he's a pro prospect. Yes, he should receive every award and citation that's available. However, those are symbols of achievements of the *past*. Scouts are paid to find talented youngsters who will produce in the *future*.

Does that mean that a player who hits .400 in college wouldn't hit well at least in Class A ball?

If Class A ball were the same as the major leagues, scouting would be much easier, because many ballplayers who hit well in college could probably hit well in Class A or Rookie League ball. But scouts are looking to sign future major leaguers, not Class A players, and that distinction is important. The question is not whether a youngster is good enough to play Class A, but whether he can someday play in the big leagues.

A Job Interview

When you play ball in front of a scout, you're really auditioning for a job, much in the same way that young actors, dancers, or musicians audition for their jobs. You've probably heard the old line that "there's a light for every broken heart on Broadway." Like Broadway, baseball is a very competitive business, and getting signed to a pro contract is not easy.

Suppose you went to a job interview at the XYZ Corporation. At the conclusion of the interview, you walk out, feeling that you put your best foot forward, answered all the questions intelligently, and presented yourself well. But a week or two later, you find out that the job went to somebody else. Understandably upset, you call the executive who interviewed you. He listens to you express your disappointment and then says, "Yes, we thought you were very good, but we found somebody we thought fit into our long-range plans even better."

It is important for you to understand that playing professional baseball is just that: a profession, a job, a career. A scout is paid by a ballclub not just to reward nice guys who had a good year in high school or college, but to find talented young men who can make solid contributions to the ballclub's future. That's why the scout's second evaluation, of future performance, is so important. He must decide just how good a youngster will be in a few years. Will he get even better, or has he already peaked?

It is not uncommon for a professional scout to draft a college ballplayer who is playing second-string to a player who, ironically, is not considered a pro prospect. In the college coach's eyes, the first-stringer is right now the better player, and the scout would likely agree with that evaluation. But in terms of long-range potential, the scout sees that the second-stringer will be bigger, stronger, quicker, and even smarter than the current guy in the lineup. From that perspective, the scout sees that present-day second-stringer as a future professional player.

Sometimes a scout may suspect that a player is playing out of position. The case of Roberto Hernandez is intriguing because as a freshman at the University of Connecticut, Hernandez was the starting catcher. He was very solid behind the plate, mainly because he was a good athlete and had a strong arm. But Roberto had always wanted to pitch; realizing that the coach at UConn needed him more as a receiver than a pitcher, Roberto decided to transfer to another school. It turned out to be an excellent move.

Last year, at the University of South Carolina (Aiken), I saw Hernandez pitch. He had not only great velocity (90 mph), but also excellent poise on the mound, and I felt he had great major league potential as a pitcher. He was drafted in the first round by the Angels.

The 20–80 Scale

Although scouting is a subjective process, many major league clubs have adopted quantitative scales to rate players' abilities. Many clubs rate a player's talents on a scale of 20 to 80, with 20 being the lowest and 80 representing all-star ability. Keep in mind, however, that this scale is based upon major league standards; that is, the prospect is being judged on how well he would stack up against current major league competition.

That is the frame of reference for scouts as they evaluate talent: How well would this player do if he were playing against big leaguers? For example, a scout might rate an outstanding high school hitter as a 30 on the scale. That means, in the scout's estimation, if this youngster were to be signed right now, he would probably hit as well as a weaker hitter in the American League, around .230.

But from the future-potential point of view, the scout might visualize this player developing into a topflight major league hitter. The scout believes that with a few years of maturation and development, that youngster could be projected as a 60. That would place him in the ranks of the better hitters in the American League; the scout's guess is that he'd be in the .290–.310 range.

Such a rating system is vitally important; it is described in Figure 4.1. A typical 17-year-old, while he might be outstanding for a high school player, wouldn't be ready even for good Class A pitching, much less major league competition. That's why he scores so low in terms of present ability. But he may appear to have big league star potential five or six years from now, and thus rate high marks for that second evaluation.

Figure 4.1.

Typical Team Grading System

Standard Grading

It is vital that each person involved in player acquisition thoroughly understands the standards by which grades are assigned when evaluating a free agent player or potential draftee. This understanding will affect consistency and uniformity in reporting, which are most important to our scouting program.

It is essential to understand EXACTLY what each numerical grade and its accurate description mean. Ratings of 60-arm, or 60-fastball, or 60-speed are EXACTLY the same in Troy, Georgia, as in Los Angeles, California.

When you say a youngster has a 50-fastball in the PRESENT category and a 60-fastball for FUTURE, you are telling us that his fastball is average compared to that of an average major league pitcher. But you project him to have an above-average fastball in the future, and thereby qualify him in the same category as a major league pitcher with an above-average fastball.

(Cont.)

Figure 4.1 (Cont.)

The same holds true for every category of evaluation. Please keep in mind that PRESENT means *now* in the major leagues and FUTURE means when the player realizes his maximum potential in the major leagues.

Guidelines for Grading

There are certain guidelines that you must adhere to for us to have a productive and meaningful system. The guidelines by which we will work are these:

A. We will grade *all* players by major league standards only. You are not to grade any player on the basis that he is the best of what you are seeing at the time.

B. All players must be assigned both PRESENT and FUTURE grades.

Rating Key

Numerical grade	Word description	Comments
80	Outstanding	The very best. Top quality.
70–79	Very good	Below outstanding but better than above average.
60–69	Above average	Below very good but better than average. Still a quality player.
50–59	Average	Right in the middle. Still some value.
40–49	Below average	Player has uncertain value.
30–39	Well below average	Only a mildly interesting player.
20–29	Poor	Weakest of all prospects. Interest based only on needs.

Present and Future Grades

As you will be grading high school and college players, it is likely that your PRESENT ratings will be below the average major league standard. Numerical grades of 20, 30, 40, and an occasional 50 or 60 could very well fit into that same evaluation. Because of your ability to project a player's skills overall after he gains some experience in professional baseball, the FUTURE grades should be coming in line with those of established major league players. There should be numerical grades in the FUTURE category of 40 and 50 and, in some cases, 60 and 70. Remember that when you are looking at high school and college players, you must grade them on major league standards, both for PRESENT and FUTURE.

To clarify, let's compare again two youngsters; one was signed, one was not. The player who went unsigned was viewed by the scouts as a 30 now, and was projected as only a 40 in the future, despite solid past credentials. That would rank him below the average major leaguer, and thus not a good prospect for signing. On the other hand, the youngster who was signed—despite lower current statistics—was only a 20 or 25, but the scouts see him developing into a 60 in a few years. Thus, he's a better prospect, and worth signing—even though right now the other kid plays better.

Playing the Detective

What are the criteria in a scout's evaluation of a player's potential development? Most scouts consider a host of items. Here's a sample:

- Size (Will he grow some more? Are his parents tall?)
- Weight (Will he get heavier in a few years?)
- Body build (Has he filled out already?)
- Strength (Has he reached his total body strength yet?)
- Body type (Are his limbs lean and long, or bulked up with muscles?)
- Running speed (Will he get any faster or slower?)
- Health (Does he have a history of being hurt? Is he just coming off an injury?)
- Emotional maturity (Could he handle the rigors of pro ball?)

Only after an extensive analysis of a young man's physical and psychological history will I make a judgment of his professional potential. In the process, I will have talked with the player's coach, friends, teammates, parents, guidance counselor, coaches from other teams, umpires who have seen him, even his girlfriend if possible—all in the pursuit of getting to know this young man and what makes him tick and, most importantly, what he'll be like in a few years.

Even after that extensive investigation, developments can take place that were impossible to predict. For example, as a senior pitcher in Royal Oaks, Michigan, lefty Brad Havens stood a mere 5'9", but because he had a strong, lively fastball, he was scouted and signed by Nick Kamzic of the Angels. In the next few months, Havens grew another three inches, and changed from a marginal prospect to a bona fide major leaguer on the way up.

Nobody could have foreseen such rapid growth, which is what makes scouting so difficult. A similar story can be told about Stanley Jefferson, a top outfield prospect for San Diego. As a high school player in New York City,

Figure 4.2.

Prospect Follow Report

Rating Key

8–Outstanding
7–Very good
6–Above average
5–Average
4–Below average
3–Well below average
2–Poor

Nonpitchers	Present	Future
Hitting ability	3	5
Power	3	5
Running speed	2	2
Base running	3	4
Arm strength	5	6
Arm accuracy	4	5
Fielding	4	5
Range	4	5
Baseball instinct	5	6
Aggressiveness	5	6
Habits	Good	
Dedication	Excellent	
Agility	Good	
Aptitude	Excellent	
Physical maturity	Good	
Emotional maturity	Good	

Stanley was fairly thin and frail, with little upper body development. But a few years later, after attending Bethune-Cookman College, Jefferson filled out, gained strength, and become a solid prospect.

These descriptions may make scouting sound like detective work, and in many ways it is. A scout is looking for any clues or hints that will help him make an accurate evaluation of a ballplayer and his potential. Many of the best scouts in baseball today actually do police or detective work as full-time occupations. Two examples are Herb Stein of the Minnesota Twins and Fred Goodman of the Pittsburgh Pirates: Both are excellent in tracking down all perspectives of a prospect.

Interpreting the 20–80 Scale

Good scouts rate all aspects of a prospect, including such basic criteria as speed, strength, size, power, hitting ability, arm strength, accuracy, and control. These and other factors are outlined in the next chapter.

Every major league club has its own way of rating players. I prefer the 20–80 scale. Other teams use a scale like the one shown in Figure 4.2. Whatever tool is used, the prospect is gauged according to current major league standards.

I'll use Gary Pettis, an Angels centerfielder, as an example. In the category of arm strength when throwing from the outfield, Gary is a 50, about average for a major leaguer.

In my travels as a scout, I might spot a youngster who also rates a 50 on throwing strength from the outfield. That rating means that if you were to take that youngster and put him in centerfield alongside Gary Pettis in Anaheim Stadium, they would have equal arm strength on their throws.

Finding such a prospect would, of course, be rare. Few young outfielders throw with even average major league strength. A high school senior able to throw as a 50 would most likely be considered as having a phenomenal cannon of an arm compared to his current teammates.

But scouts do rate some prospects with high scores. Consider Bo Jackson of Auburn, a Heisman Trophy winner. Bo started his professional baseball career on very shaky ground, and fans were asking how in the world this guy could be considered a future major leaguer. After all, he was hitting less than his weight and striking out just about every other at bat. But if you saw Bo's ratings, you'd realize that he had been chosen based on his potential as a player, not necessarily what he could do right now.

Specifically, the Major League Scouting Bureau graded Jackson's potential baseball skills at 75.5 (out of 80). Anyone rated over 70 is considered to be in the superstar category. Only time will tell whether Bo performs as well as predicted, but the scouts obviously felt that he has all the tools to be a great player.

Chapter 5

The Fundamental Ingredients of a Major League Ballplayer

A scout who comes to watch and evaluate a ballplayer has been trained to look beyond the player's game performance on that particular day. He also studies the various components of the player's game—the physical and psychological factors that distinguish the abilities of one ballplayer from those of another.

There are five fundamental physical tools, or skills, that scouts look for when evaluating talent. As I mentioned in the previous chapter, the scout not only wants to see you do well in the game he's watching, he also is there to analyze your *potential* as a professional ballplayer. To do that, he must carefully check your physical tools.

Scouts also analyze your "mental tools." You'll learn how important those are in a later section of this chapter, "Scouting the Intangibles." A comprehensive description of what scouts evaluate as they observe ballplayers is also included in this chapter. Read this material very carefully: It could hold the key to a professional contract.

Physical Tools

Arm Strength

This is a tool often overlooked by many young ballplayers. But having a strong arm, whether from the outfield, infield, or behind the plate, is essential. Particularly these days, when so many major league games are played on artificial turf, an infielder plays deeper and must rely on a strong arm to throw swift runners out. The same is true for an outfielder, who has to track balls down and fire shots to the infield to keep runners from advancing. And a catcher has to be able to get rid of the ball in a hurry to throw out potential base stealers.

Thus, if you're going to show a scout your true abilities, when you throw during infield/outfield practice you must be warmed up and throw the ball with your full strength. If you throw halfheartedly or just lob the ball, a scout can only assume that your arm is either weak, injured, or substandard. If he comes to that conclusion, you have eliminated one category by which you could be added to his follow-up list.

Hitting Ability

When I scout a hitter, I'm looking for his ability

- to make contact with the ball
- to hit the ball hard

- to swing the bat quickly (bat speed)
- to hit to all fields
- to be aggressive at the plate
- to make adjustments if fooled on a pitch
- to make the ball "jump off" the bat

Jumping off the bat is an expression that reflects how hard the ball has been hit. A youngster may bat .400 by hitting lots of flares, loops, "seeing-eye" ground balls, or bunts. While there's no denying that he hit .400, there is no evidence that he hits the ball hard. A scout looks for a ballplayer who consistently hits the ball hard; that's a telltale sign of a good professional hitter.

Fielding Ability

A scout looks for quick hands, soft hands, and quick feet. He will tell you that it's not enough just to be able to field a ball well. He looks for a ballplayer's ability

- to cover a large area of the infield and outfield (range)
- to move, or jump, on the ball before it is hit (quick feet)
- to receive the ball with little effort and with smoothness and grace (soft hands)
- to move his hands quickly in fielding a bad hop (quick hands)
- to get his feet set smoothly to make the throw
- to play gracefully (Does he make a difficult play look easy?)

Some players have limited running speed, but fielding instincts that give them quickness. Good scouts see that quickness. Graig Nettles and Brooks Robinson, great defensive third basemen, were never considered fast runners, but their fielding quickness allowed them to cover all sorts of ground. Remember: Quickness is not the same as speed.

Hitting With Power

Most baseball fans assume that hitting with power means hitting a ball 400 feet or more. Although raw home-run power is a major component of power-hitting, some players specialize in hitting hard, powerful line drives. For example, Pete Rose, even during his prime, was not considered a home-run hitter. But that doesn't mean he didn't hit with power.

For every home-run hitter in the majors, there are plenty of guys who are there not to hit homers, but because they hit the ball powerfully. There is a definite difference. As far as your performance is concerned, work to hit the ball consistently hard, and let the scouts judge how well you hit.

Running Speed

Of all a player's physical tools, running speed is the easiest to judge. A stopwatch and a 60-yard dash are all you need to determine how fast (or slow) a ballplayer is. However, if pure speed were all that mattered, plenty of track stars would make great base runners. Scouts know that speed has to be utilized properly on the base paths to be effective and that many players rely on instinct and quickness to overcome a lack of foot speed.

Once a ballplayer is labeled slow, the label tends to stick. But some "slow" ballplayers run the base paths much faster than their speedier teammates, because they run the bases better, or know how to round a base or get a good jump off a pitcher. Again, scouts are aware of these realities. You can understand, though, that a scout would prefer to sign a player who runs well.

Can you make yourself faster as you get older? It may be possible. An example is B.J. Surhoff, who was the first pick in the nation in 1985, out of the University of North Carolina. B.J. was not considered particularly fleet-footed in high school. Yet as he matured physically, B.J. found that his speed increased, and he stole quite a few bases in college. In other words, as he got older, he got faster.

When Wade Boggs was starting out in the minor leagues, he too was considered slow, being clocked down to first at 4.3 or 4.4 seconds. Wade worked hard to improve his running speed; one day, in 1982, he consulted with some local track coaches. The coaches agreed that Wade's running style was all wrong: He was running heel-to-toe instead of on the balls of his feet. They gave him a program to improve his style, and then he worked every day to consciously change his running method. Wade now runs to first from home in 4.15 seconds—only average for the major leagues, but no longer slow.

"Major League Ability"

When I scout a player, I analyze him according to the five physical tools that have been described. If a player has average major league ability in just two of the five categories, then he's automatically a prospect I follow up on.

"Average major league ability" means a player currently has skills as good as those of an average major leaguer. Suppose a youngster has great speed and a great throw from the outfield; he's good enough to be rated as a 50 in both speed and arm strength. That means he's considered as good as an average major leaguer in those two categories. That youngster deserves to be followed.

I must point out that it's rare to find a high school player who rates a 50 for current ability in any category. For example, when I saw Darryl Strawberry, a Mets' slugger, play at Crenshaw High School in Los Angeles, I rated him as a 25 hitter with a potential of 70. It's tough to be rated that highly by a scout, particularly when you're being compared to big leaguers.

But by the same token, remember that as you develop, you'll need at least two of the five criteria to be a prospect. However, many major league players aren't rated as 50s in all categories. Two good shortstops come to mind: Both Larry Bowa and Buddy Harrelson were probably rated only 25 or 30 for their hitting and their power.

However, both rated very highly in running, fielding, and throwing. Based on their scores in those areas, they were not only scouted and signed, but also advanced to the major leagues and were topflight players for years.

My point is that you need to show the scouts that you do have some ability, whether it's running speed, arm strength, or hitting power. Just show it once, and the good scout will follow up on it.

What Scouts Look For in Pitchers

So far most of my advice for playing in front of a scout has been directed to position players, that is, infielders, outfielders, and catchers. The remaining players—pitchers—aren't allowed to do much during the pregame workout. They may shag flies or hit grounders to the infielders or throw a little batting practice. But for the most part, pitchers can only show their stuff in a game or warming up on the sidelines before their turn in the rotation.

I'll often follow a starting pitcher out to the bull pen to watch him warm up. A scout can learn quite a bit about a pitching prospect just by watching him throw on the side. Specifically, the scout can see whether the pitcher has much velocity, a good breaking pitch, a smooth mechanical action, good control, and so on.

A scout can't judge a pitcher merely by the way he throws in the bull pen, but the scout can get a preview of what the pitcher wants to display in the game. Does his ball have any movement to it? What about his move from the stretch? Does he have a third, or strikeout, pitch?

The scout may get an idea of a pitcher's maturity and experience by seeing how he warms up. Does he do any stretching or calisthenics first? Does he start throwing from a short distance or a long one? While coaching plays a vital role in helping a pitcher learn the fundamentals of warming up, from the scout's perspective it's how you personally decide to prepare for a game that is most important.

A good scout does homework on a pitcher to find out basic information such as height, weight, and age, as well as to learn about any arm injuries and the last time he pitched or played in a game. Particularly at the high school level, where the best pitcher might play another position on days that he's not pitching, this kind of information is important.

Here's a good example to illustrate: I scouted Dwight Gooden as a high school senior in Tampa and clocked him at 81 mph. That's certainly a decent speed for a high school pitcher, but was nowhere near the kind of velocity that "Dr. K" normally generated. I wanted to find out why Dwight was throwing 10 to 15 mph less than usual. Some investigation turned up the answer: The day before, Dwight had played third base and had quite a few plays in the field, many of them testing his arm. As a result, his velocity on the mound the next day was lessened. If I hadn't asked why Dwight wasn't throwing in the 90s, I might have greatly underrated his arm strength.

When observing a prospect, a scout evaluates several key components of pitching. Some of these are obvious ingredients, some are more subtle, but the experienced scout checks to see how a pitching prospect rates on each particular aspect.

1. Velocity: Perhaps the most obvious of all pitching components, a scout first considers the amount of force, or velocity, with which a pitcher throws. A typical velocity rating scale is shown in Table 5.1.
2. Movement: Just as important as velocity is the ball's movement. Does the pitcher's ball sink, drop, slide, fade, rise, or merely go straight? The scout is usually more interested in a pitcher's ball that has more movement.
3. General mechanics: Does the pitcher exhibit the expected amounts of maturity, poise, rhythm, and pitching techniques on the mound?
4. Delivery: Specifically, the scout considers the pitcher's release point. Is the pitcher's delivery over-the-top, three-quarters, sidearm, or submarine? Is it free and fluid or forced and labored?
5. Arm action: Is the pitcher getting the full extension on his arm when he releases the ball? Is his motion herky-jerky or fluid? In other words, does his delivery make him suspect for an arm injury?

Table 5.1 Rating Pitching Velocity

Grades (20–80 scale)	=	MPH
80	=	98 +
70-79	=	93–97
60-69	=	90–92
50-59	=	88–89
40-49	=	85–87
30-39	=	83–84
20-29	=	Below 82

6. Curve ball: When evaluating the pitcher's curve, scouts check for rotation, sharpness, the direction in which it breaks (down, across, or both), and how much it breaks (a few inches or closer to a foot?). Can a batter easily adjust to the pitch or does the pitcher hide it well in the wind-up?

7. Other pitches: What other pitches can the pitcher throw and control? These might include slider, knuckleball, screwball, forkball, palmball, or splitfinger fastball.

8. Change-up: The off-speed pitch is considered vital for success in professional baseball. If a pitcher is able to throw a change-up, the scouts want to know how often he can use it effectively.

9. Control: Also vitally important for success; scouts gauge whether control allows a pitcher to pinpoint certain pitches, or if the pitcher is just learning how to find the plate.

10. Type: The scouts label pitchers as certain types. Is a pitcher overpowering with a blazing fastball, a finesse pitcher who just hits the corners on the plate, or a mix pitcher with a combination of good fastball, curve, and change-up?

A pitcher must have a sound delivery, good basics, and good arm action or must show that some minor adjustment will give him these qualities in the near future. Bad arm action, poor delivery, or both will considerably lessen the chances of a young pitcher improving his potential enough to be projected by scouts as a prospect. Experience shows that scouts can look for improvements with breaking pitches, changes of speed, and control. Even the fastball can improve with time.

Pitchers and Their Arms

If a scout is watching you play and you have an arm injury or are coming off one, make certain he knows about it. Remember, a scout can pass judgment only on what he sees. If you enter a game to pitch or play, he can only assume that you're healthy. If you're not at 100%, ask your coach to let the scout know your condition.

Before the action begins at tryout camps, scouts always ask for kids who are slightly injured or have just thrown in a game the day before to speak up. But many kids have learned to think that complaining about injuries is not "macho." Rather than saying that he pitched nine innings the day before or that he has an injured elbow or a muscle spasm in his back, the typical youngster will grab the ball and head to the mound or the field.

The irony of this scenario is that the youngster invariably does not have a good outing, and as a result, gets crossed off the follow-up list. That can be a double loss—for the player, who should have said that he was tired or hurt, and for the scout, who can only make his judgment by what a youngster shows him.

What Scouts Look For in Catchers

Catchers have to represent a combination of strength, durability, intelligence, arm accuracy, and if possible, good hitting ability. Such combinations are rare; hence, a good catching prospect is a great find. When looking at a catching prospect, scouts check the following key components.

1. Arm strength: First and foremost, does the catcher have a good, solid throw to second base? Is there potential for that arm strength to improve?
2. Release: Does the catcher have strong wrist action? That is, can he get rid of the ball in a hurry without having to wind up his entire arm?
3. Accuracy: A strong arm isn't the only ability a catcher needs. Can he throw the ball directly to second base on a straight line, time and time again without missing the mark?
4. Hands: Does the catcher have hands that gently receive the pitch, or does he fight the pitch as it comes to the plate? The "softer" the receiver, the better the prospect.
5. Agility: Is the catcher good at moving around the plate? Can he easily block balls in front of the plate? Can he track down pop-ups fairly well? Is he good at getting out in front of the plate to handle bunts?

6. Leadership: Does the catcher show the kind of field leadership that he needs to exhibit? Does he call the pitches, or does the coach? Can he communicate well and calm down the pitcher when things get rough?

What Scouts Look For in Infielders

The two most important tools an infielder can have are "quick feet" and "soft hands"—the ability to gracefully field a ground ball as though it's a thoroughly natural, unhurried event. Although many scouts feel that this skill really can't be taught, that the ability is inborn, the more practice you get at fielding grounders, the better you'll become. A scout will look at the following components to find a good infielder.

1. Range: An infielder must move quickly in all directions. This includes not only going to one's right or left to make a play, but also to backpeddle into the outfield as well as to charge a slow roller.
2. Quick feet: Especially for those plays around second base on a pivot, an infielder must exhibit quick feet along with agility and athletic skill.
3. Arm strength: Like the other defensive positions in the field, an infielder must show a strong, accurate arm. Because so many major league ballparks have artificial turf, infielders must play deeper than normal; this places a higher premium on a strong arm.
4. Taking charge: Infielders tend to be involved in almost every play. Scouts look for an infielder's leadership abilities to see how he "takes charge" on the field. This might include taking time to talk with the pitcher, letting the outfielders know how many outs there are, directing traffic on crucial plays, etc.
5. Aggressiveness: In line with taking charge, scouts appreciate an infielder who is aggressive in his play, who is not afraid to hang tough on a pivot play or to knock down a hard-hit grounder.

What Scouts Look For in Outfielders

Outfielders tend to be regarded by some fans as offensively oriented players, but scouts know that swinging the bat is only part of the outfielder's job. Arm strength, defensive skills, and speed, as well as several other skills, are critical parts of the outfielder's game.

1. Arm strength: The strongest arm in the outfield usually belongs to the right fielder because he has to make the longest throws. But

scouts want to make sure that the center fielder and left fielder have good, solid arm strength as well as accuracy and quick release.

2. Jump: When a ball is hit, a good outfielder automatically gets a "jump" on the ball; he gets into position to make the next play as the pitch makes contact with the bat. Some scouts feel that this ability, like others, is more of an instinct than a trait that can be learned, but the more one practices catching fly balls, the more one can improve.

3. Fielding ground balls: Being an outfielder doesn't exclude a player from handling grounders. The ability to cleanly pick up a ball hit to the outfield, without bobbling it, is an essential part of outfield play.

4. Handling the terrain: Can the outfielder range in all directions well? Does he know how to go back on a ball, how to use the warning track, and how to play a ball off the wall?

5. Steps: When throwing the ball back to the infield, does the outfielder position himself to get the most out of his throws? Does he release the ball quickly? Does he take only a couple of steps in his release?

6. Speed: Can the outfielder use his speed in covering territory? Does he know how to cut a ball off before it gets to the gap? Does he know how to charge a sinking line drive without being "handcuffed"?

What Scouts Look For in Base Runners

Base running is an art form that too many ballplayers overlook. Speed is definitely an added bonus for running the bases, but it's hardly the only requirement. A ballplayer who possesses average speed can be an outstanding base runner as long as he has the proper instincts on the bases.

1. Overall speed: Speed is a terrific asset to have as a base runner. A player who can run well should certainly exhibit that speed whenever possible, whether hustling down the first baseline, on the bases, or in the field.

2. Quickness: Not to be confused with raw speed, quickness refers to a runner's first few steps. Some runners, even those who don't possess great speed, are particularly good at getting a quick start on the bases.

3. Instincts: Scouts like to see a base runner who is daring and aggressive on the bases. That doesn't mean taking foolish risks, but

rather knowing when to steal a base, how to slide, how to take an extra base on a base hit, and so on. Again, the solid base runner can couple his speed, quickness, and instincts to make himself a threat on the bases.

4. Sliding ability: Scouts check the mechanics of sliding, including the standard bent-leg slide, the hook slide, the evasive slide (i.e., sliding away from the base to avoid a tag, and then reaching back with the hand), and the head-first slide.

5. Coaching signals: A base runner, while running the bases, must have the ability to see his third base coach and to find the ball on a hit-and-run or straight steal play. Scouts don't like base runners who run with their heads down; finding the ball is essential to becoming a professional base runner.

What Scouts Look For in Hitters

Scouts know that there are different kinds of hitters, such as long-distance hitters, contact, line-drive hitters, and slap hitters. As Ted Williams has said many times, hitting is the most difficult task in all sports. Once you've found a hitting style that makes you feel comfortable, stay with it and keep working on it. In the meantime, the scouts will evaluate your hitting strengths and potential.

1. Type of stroke: Scouts first classify what kind of stroke a hitter has, whether it's short and compact, long and looping, quick, etc. The fact that there is no perfect stroke should not discourage prospective hitters.

2. Faults: Scouts also immediately check out any flaws a hitter may have in his stroke. Those flaws include hitching, overstriding, bailing out on curves, and dropping the back shoulder. While these flaws can all be corrected, a scout must first be aware of them.

3. Type of hitter: There are many kinds of hitters, as identified in the following complete checklist: aggressive (free swinger), defensive (takes a lot of pitches), power hitter (home-run swinger), spray or singles hitter (short stroke), line-drive, pull hitter, straight away, opposite field, and hitter to all fields.

4. Power: Power is not restricted to home-run hitters. Scouts know that a line-drive hitter can put as much power into his stroke as a home-run hitter. Scouts want to see the ball "jump" off the bat; They're not interested in weak line drives or soft fly balls. They want to see how the batter hits the ball, which is the key to judging a hitter's power.

5. Bunting: Bunting seems to be a lost art, so if a hitter can bunt for a hit or put down a good sacrifice bunt, that will impress the scouts. A left-handed hitter with good speed should possess the drag bunt as a vital part of his repertoire. Too many kids avoid working on bunting skills; make sure you don't.

But What About My Stats?

Many scouts regard statistics as an indicator not so much of professional ability, but rather of potential strengths and weaknesses. That's something that many players, and their parents, don't understand.

When I look at a ballplayer's stat sheet, I'm looking for trends and subtle indices. For example, if a prospect is supposed to be a fleet-footed second baseman, I check to see how many stolen bases he has—and just as important, how many times he got caught stealing.

I look to see whether he leads his team in triples; if he's truly that fast on the bases, he should be able to stretch a few doubles. I look at his on-base percentage: a guy with great speed has to be on base to be a positive force on his team offensively. I also check his ratio of walks to strikeouts; a player with top speed should have plenty of walks and ideally few strikeouts.

Whether a prospect hits .250 or .400 is not necessarily as important as these other stats. Of course, if a player is truly top-notch, all of his stats will be glittering. But many times a scout can find a less obvious diamond in the rough simply by reading between the lines of the stat sheet.

A few years ago there was a catcher, Chris Jelic, out of the University of Pittsburgh who, although he didn't have the highest batting average on his squad, did have plenty of doubles, triples, and home runs. A football player, Chris was hefty, and the power he showed during the baseball season convinced the Kansas City Royals that if he had an opportunity to concentrate solely on baseball, his power and skills might be awesome. Based on his future potential and his slugging percentage statistics, the Royals made him a high draft choice.

Stats, though, are never a guarantee that an individual will be a first-round draft choice, or a prospect at all. Dan Quisenberry had an outstanding record and ERA as a pitcher at LaVerne College in California. And his record was no fluke; his senior year stats were as good as his junior year accomplishments.

However, despite his top-notch collegiate career, Quiz never threw harder than 75 mph. Though he was effective against other college players, most pro scouts didn't project Dan as a bona fide major league prospect because he just didn't throw hard enough and, being in his early 20s, probably never would throw any harder.

As a result, Quisenberry was bypassed in the professional draft. Eventually, after checking around with various scouts, he finally got a shot with the Royals. He signed for a $500 bonus as a free agent, but still was not considered a real prospect until he had a few good years in the minors. Dan never did develop exceptional speed, but his unusual delivery got the job done with great movement and deception.

Quisenberry was fortunate, and his story illustrates the point that just because you aren't drafted doesn't mean you won't ever play pro ball. You have to stay after it. There are plenty of stories like that of Dan Quisenberry. Pete Rose signed for a $500 bonus; obviously, the major league teams weren't falling over themselves to bid for his services, even though he had put together some great high school statistics in Cincinnati.

Another example of misleading stats involves Bo Jackson. When he was a freshman outfielder at Auburn, he struck out his first 21 times at bat! Naturally, if you were going just by his batting average and number of strikeouts, you might write Bo off. But from a scout's point of view, he had so many potential major league tools that despite his poor showing at the plate, Bo was followed all through his college career.

My point is that statistics can provide good insight for analysis, but a scout never relies solely on a player's stat sheet in deciding whether to offer a possible contract. Understanding that should give a player more insight into who qualifies as a prospect.

The role of statistics in baseball was summed up well by famed commentator Vin Scully, who said, "Stats are used by baseball fans in much the same way that a drunk leans against a street lamp; it's there more for support than for enlightenment." That same analogy could be applied to the use of statistics by scouts.

Scouting the Intangibles

Of all the variables in scouting a prospect, the most difficult aspects to gauge accurately are the intangibles: a player's psychological makeup, motivation, future physical changes, and other traits that are not readily apparent. Some kids are blessed with all the physical tools to become great major leaguers, but they just don't have the burning desire to compete. On the other hand are ballplayers who are only fringe prospects because of their limited physical abilities, but who overcome those drawbacks by squeezing the very most out of their limited potential.

These psychological variables help make scouting challenging as well as rewarding. For every first-round, number-one, "can't-miss" pick in the nation, there's another kid who doesn't get drafted, but does everything he possibly can to get signed and then fights his way through the minors to the big leagues.

Making predictions about a ballplayer's intangibles—his desire to succeed—is the most difficult part of a scout's job. That's one reason a scout will come back to see a good player again and again, in hopes of finding out a bit more about his psyche and motivation.

If a scout is watching a youngster, and the player does well that day, both the player and the scout are happy. But the savvy scout wants to be there on the day that the prospect strikes out four times in a row or gets shelled in the first inning. Seeing how a young prospect reacts to adversity can give a scout an entirely different perspective on what makes him tick.

It's easy to smile and be cordial when things are going well. The scout wants to know if a prospect can react positively to bad days as well. As a player in the minor leagues, you sleep in cheap hotels, take long bus rides, eat fast food, face intense competition, and play in mediocre ballparks. Nobody is there to hold your hand or to reassure you if you have a bad day or go into a slump. You're on your own, competing and scratching your way to the top.

If a scout can see how a youngster handles himself in negative situations on the field today, he has a better idea of how that player will handle life in the minors tomorrow.

The Psychological Makeup of a Player

Many modern-day scouts would readily say that a ballplayer's psychological makeup contributes heavily to determining what kind of prospect he'll be. A scout first has to find a player with the necessary physical tools. But then he has to make certain that the prospect has the right psychological tools as well.

Why is the psychological aspect so important? One reason is that nearly every player who is drafted and signed has to report to the minor leagues before he can realistically be considered for a major league club roster.

Scouts need to sign players who can handle the arduous lifestyle of the minors. It's one thing to be a star baseball player at the hometown high school or local junior college. But what happens when a youngster is placed in a town hundreds of miles from his family and friends? Suddenly he's on his own, and he has to produce against the best pitching or hitting he's ever faced.

Some kids, even ones with great potential, just can't adjust to the minor league lifestyle, and they pack it in and try another profession. To help guard against that, most clubs have guidelines like the ones in Figure 5.1 for scouts to help newly signed players.

Figure 5.1.

Guiding the Signed Player

Individual Player Items

A very important part of the interpersonal nature of any signing is a genuine interest that you, our scout and field representative, show in the player. Many scouts feel that their job has ended once the signing has been completed. We in the _____ organization do not subscribe to that belief.

At this point, in addition to inspecting the numbers and conditions of the player's equipment, you should advise him about the personal belongings to bring on what may be his very first trip away from home. Make suggestions from your own experience and from recent signings. Use your involvement in professional ball to help youngsters with some of their personal needs. As a guideline you might include the following:

Four or five pairs of slacks and dress jeans
A pair or two of dungarees or chino pants
One or two pairs of shorts
Underwear (six sets)
Socks (athletic and regular)
Toiletries
A sweater or two
Seven or eight collar shirts (plus T-shirts)
At least one suit or a couple of sports jackets (and two or three ties)
A pair of sneakers
A couple pairs of shoes and sandals
A raincoat (depending on the part of the country)

(Cont.)

Figure 5.1 (Cont.)

Instruct the young player to carry his baseball equipment on the plane with him and that he can check his personal clothing items through to his final destination. With regard to the question of how much money to bring, our organization suggests that you advise the family that $100 in cash is enough. The player should also bring a check for $100–$200 so that he can start a checking account in the town where he will be playing summer ball.

Player Equipment

Each scout performs an important inspection of the condition and amount of equipment that a newly signed player owns upon his reporting to begin his professional baseball career.

Our ballclub may spend thousands of dollars to scout a player and then thousands more if he is signed. Yet some players are allowed to report for their professional baseball education with equipment that is lacking in numbers and substandard in grade.

When this happens, we are guilty of poor follow-through in signing a player. We also allow ourselves to use poor public relations procedures. To eliminate these problems and, more importantly, to better serve the new player and help him get started on the right foot, the home office asks each scout to do the following with regard to equipment and to advise the player accordingly.

1. Ask the player to show you every piece of equipment he has. List the items, and evaluate the condition of each piece of equipment.
2. Recommend that the new player have the following equipment when he leaves home to report for his first pro ball assignment:
   a. Two pairs of spikes (both should be broken in)
   b. Two gloves (one good one; the other can be old)
   c. At least four sweatshirts (weight of material to be dictated by the part of the country player is reporting to)
   d. At least two athletic supporters and cups
   e. A jacket (windbreaker preferably): A MUST FOR ALL PITCHERS.

Note: Many high school players still use heavy basketball sweatsocks under their stockings. Please discourage this—players will be issued sanitary stockings for that purpose.

Other players somehow know what to expect, and they persevere against the odds. These are the kids who are determined to play in the big leagues, no matter how long the bus rides or how lousy the fields.

These are the kids scouts want to sign, for they have both the physical skills and the mental toughness to make the grade in this demanding profession.

Some ballclubs actually use standardized tests to gauge a prospect's psychological profile. The New York Mets administer The Athletic Motivation Inventory (AMI) to all their potential prospects.

According to Joe McIlvaine, vice president of baseball operations for the Mets, the results of the AMI are so important to their scouting reports that unless a prospect scores well, he won't be considered, no matter how physically talented he might be. The test has no right or wrong answers; it merely measures an athlete's competitive personality. There are multiple-choice questions; a player's answers are analyzed by computer. The player is rated on characteristics such as mental toughness, leadership tendencies, and coachability.

This particular exam has been used by at least 14 major league clubs, as well as by teams in the National Basketball Association, the National Hockey League, and the National Football League. A team scouting you is likely to ask that you take a psychological test of some kind, such as the AMI.

A formal psychological examination is one means of measuring a youngster's desire to play ball. Another is observing whether a youngster works hard during pregame activities. What does he show about his "work ethic"? Does he go about his business in a serious, professional manner, or does he approach the game in a lackadaisical, careless way? Does he encourage his teammates and lead by example?

Team spirit is another important quality for a player, and scouts often casually interview a prospect's teammates to learn what kind of impression he has made on his peers. Is he popular? Well-liked? Or is he thought of as conceited and self-centered? These are additional pieces of the puzzle that a scout has to put together to judge a prospect.

Physical Changes

Though most scouts are aware that physical changes occur as a player matures, such changes are impossible to predict. B. J. Surhoff was mentioned earlier as a player whose maturation process allowed him to become faster. He's not a rarity. A pudgy youngster may lose his baby fat; a smallish shortstop may sprout by three or four inches. Such physical changes certainly do occur, and a ballplayer's abilities can be greatly enhanced.

Pete Incaviglia, the budding superstar of the Texas Rangers, was only 5'2" and 140 pounds as a sophomore in high school. Today, he's 6'1" and 200. When Mike Loynd, pitcher for the Rangers, started college at Florida State, he was 6'0" and 170 pounds. Three years later he had grown to 6'5' and 220. His growth helped strengthen his arm and improve his velocity to the plate.

So how important is one's physical image as a player? Many years ago, there was a short pudgy catcher who played in the Parade Grounds in New York City. The area was full of good players, and scouts combed the park regularly for prospects. This chubby kid was a pretty decent hitter and receiver, but because he looked so little like a professional ballplayer, the scouts never gave him much attention.

Finally, though, somebody gave him a chance in spite of his weight problem. With a few years in the minors and a strict diet, that pudgy little kid blossomed into one of the all-time great hitters of the National League, Joe Torre.

Sometimes young players complain that scouts don't pay attention to them because they're too small. Consider Brett Butler's story: When he was a junior in high school, Brett wasn't even a starter on his team. After finishing high school, this future all-star major leaguer didn't receive even one scholarship offer to play baseball.

So Brett went to Arizona State University as a walk-on, nonscholarship player and ended up on the junior varsity squad. Still not happy with his baseball progress, Butler transferred to Southeastern Oklahoma State University. Upon finally getting a chance to play every day, Brett hit 31 homers in three years, became a great outfielder, and made all-America teams twice.

Yet the same label that haunted Brett Butler through high school and college plagued him at the start of his pro career. Even the scouts thought he might be "too small" to play in the major leagues, and thus Brett was drafted on the 23rd round and signed for just $1,000.

Once he got his chance in pro ball, though, Butler skyrocketed through the minors to stardom in the big leagues. Brett is indeed a small player—barely 5'9" and about 160 pounds—yet he persisted until he got a chance.

Evaluating Your Strengths and Weaknesses

The scout's job is to serve *every player* on the field, so he gathers information on each one. Most amateur teams carry at most twenty guys, and about twelve actually play. So a scout has to keep track of up to forty guys a game, but may get notes on only two dozen.

Many scouts make rough notes on a form similar to the one in Figure 5.2. For a final analysis, or after seeing a player more than once, a scout would complete the form again according to the instructions in "Explanation and Formula for Grading."

Figure 5.2 can be an important tool for your self-evaluation, because it lists specifics of what a scout is looking for. Make copies of these forms and write your own "report card" in comparison to what the scouts are seeking. Then work on the areas where you are weakest, and exploit ones in which you excel.

The final section of this chapter provides some basic tips for improving your skills.

A Scout's Tips for Improving Your Skills

While there's no question that professional baseball players are blessed with certain physical skills, there's also no question that an individual ballplayer can constantly improve upon his abilities and enhance his performance on the field. To that end, the following section contains several tips on how you can improve certain parts of your game. However, these are merely offered as suggestions; you should also talk with your coaches and read other books on the particular aspects of the game, such as hitting, fielding, and pitching.

Remember, the game of baseball is just as much a mental game as it is a physical one. Thus, the more you study the skills of baseball, the better ballplayer you're going to be. Remember that most of the skills in baseball take many weeks of hard work and development before you'll experience any noticeable improvement.

1. Hitting: You can improve your stroke by developing more upper body strength, changing your stance, shortening your stride, shortening your stroke, improving your knowledge of the strike zone, or learning how to read a pitcher.

   Wrist and forearm strength is an important component of good hitting ability. If you want to strengthen your wrists so that the ball jumps off the bat, squeeze a tennis ball repetitiously every day. In my experience, this is more beneficial than swinging a loaded bat daily. It takes a long time to see results—months, even years—but once you develop your wrists, you'll find much more punch you

Figure 5.2.

Scout's Note Form

Rating key

80–Outstanding	40–Below average
70–Very good	30–Well below average
60–Above average	20–Poor
50–Average	

Position player **Present Future** **Use rating key grades**
Show times to first and dashes

Position player	Present	Future						
Hitting	___	___	Hitch	___	Bat speed	___	Contact	___
Power	___	___	Pull	___	Alley	___	Line drive	___
Speed	___	___	To first base	___	40-yd dash	___	60-yd dash	___
Arm	___	___	Strength	___	Accuracy	___	Release	___
Field	___	___	Range	___	Hands	___	Agility	___
Base running	___	___	Instincts	___	Aggressiveness	___	Leads	___

Type hitter (circle proper category)   Power   Line drive   Slap

Player's makeup

Competitiveness	___	Intelligence	___
Confidence	___	Poise	___
Dependability	___	Teamwork	___
Honesty	___		

Pitcher	Present	Future	Use rating key grades			
Fastball	___	___	Velocity (MPH)	___	Life	___
Curve	___	___	Velocity	___	Break	___
Slider	___	___	Velocity	___	Break	___
Change	___	___	Fast ball	___	Breaking pitch	___
Other pitch	___	___	Type	___	Control	___
Control	___	___	Fastball	___	Breaking ball	___

Type pitcher (circle proper category)   Power   Sink/slide   Finesse

Player's makeup

Competitiveness	___	Intelligence	___
Confidence	___	Poise	___
Dependability	___	Teamwork	___
Honesty	___		

(Cont.)

Figure 5.2 (Cont.)

Explanation and Formula for Grading

In arriving at the total grade, only the future grades are to be used. The formula is different for the position player than for the pitcher.

For the position player you total five boxes: hitting, power, speed, arm, and fielding. Take the total of the five boxes and divide by 5.

For the pitcher, you total at the most five boxes: fastball, curve, slider, other pitch, and control. If the pitcher only shows you a fastball and curve, then you total these two plus control for three boxes. In any case, you only divide the total by the number of boxes you graded him in, and never by any more than 5.

In completing the formula, you may either upgrade or downgrade the grade after division, by anywhere from 1 to 4 points.

Example:

Position player

Ability	Present	Future
Hitting	33	47
Power	43	52
Speed	61	72
Arm	59	61
Field	52	69
		Total these grades only

The total of the future grades in this area is 301. Divide the total of 301 by 5. The overall grade to this point is 60.2. You may upgrade this player 3 points because of his superior makeup. Add these 3 points to the 60.2 and you get a total of 63.2.

Example:

Pitcher

Ability	Present	Future
Fastball	37	54
Curve	39	47
Slider	44	57
Other pitch	None	
Control	45	56
		Total these grades only

Because you evaluated this pitcher in four categories, then you divide by 4. The total of the future grades in this area is 214. Divide the total of 214 by 4. The overall grade to this point is 53.5.

Because of his makeup, you may downgrade this pitcher 3 points. Subtract these 3 points from the 53.5, and you get a total of 50.5.

can put into your swing. And the best time to start that development is while you're in high school.

2. Power: You can enhance your power at the plate by lifting weights to improve your body strength, selecting a different weight bat, improving your selection of pitches to swing at, being more aggressive when hitting, or changing your stance or stride.

3. Pitching arm: A scout might give you some exercises for improving your arm or show you how to increase your arm speed.

4. Grip: A scout might also have some suggestions for your grip on the ball when pitching or your grip on the bat when hitting. Generally, you want to hold a bat loosely across your fingers (not your palms). For pitchers, the way in which you grip the ball (across 4 seams, across 2 seams, or no seams) can very much affect the flight of the pitch.

5. Infield play: Scouts want complete ballplayers, so they might suggest ways you can polish your infield game, including your range, getting in position on ground balls, learning how to use sunglasses, and learning cut-off positions and relays.

6. Outfield play: Outfielders must know how to cover ground, get their bodies in position for a catch-and-throw play, hit cut-off men, use sunglasses, and play a ball in the gap and off the wall.

7. Catching: Key areas for improvement include your stance, your glove in position, shifting your weight, how to block a pitch, how to handle a pop-fly, pitch selection, knowledge of hitters, and how to take charge.

8. Base running: Scouts want to see if you know how to take a lead, get a good jump on a pitcher, round a base, find the ball when running on a play, if you have good instincts, and just how aggressive you are on the bases. Following are some specific steps you can take to improve running speed:

Step 1. Work on your upper-body strength by doing pull-ups, push-ups and, if available, bench presses. Shoulder and back strength are essential for leg speed.

Step 2. Work on your overall strength by engaging in a weight training program. Emphasize exercises for leg muscles—knees, hips, thighs, calves. Don't overdo it.

Step 3. When you run, start with small inclines. Gradually increase the uphill nature of the workout, like football teams do in running stadium steps.

Step 4. Alternate a pattern of jogging with wind sprints and even some distance work to build up lung capacity. Try some all-out sprints in the middle of your workout. Go 100 yards full blast, then jog the same distance, then sprint again.

Step 5. Incorporate this weight and running program into your regular workouts, so you do it consistently. Irregular workouts won't help as much. Keep track of your progress, maybe by getting an observer to time specific efforts over a six-week period. Don't be afraid to ask for professional help to improve your speed.

9. Overall arm strength: Here is a specific exercise for improving arm strength. Play catch with a friend, starting at a distance of about 60 feet. After your arm is loose, start expanding the distance gradually. Take a few steps backward after each throw, but continue to throw hard. Don't just lob the ball; throw with some zip, and throw accurately. Keep backing up until you have doubled the distance from your friend. Go back as far as you want, although eventually you'll find a limit beyond which you have to throw the ball on a hop to get it to the other player.

   Throwing at longer distances will build up your arm strength as well as your accuracy. However, to keep improving your arm strength, you must do this throwing daily, every time you practice. Doing this exercise just once in a while will limit its impact on your arm strength.

Chapter 6

Marketing Yourself: Hits and Myths

The one question asked most often by baseball fans and aspiring pro players about scouting is probably this:

Where are the best places to be scouted?

Following that query is a natural corollary: Okay, once I know where the scouts are, what can I do to make certain that they notice me?

Perhaps the best way to answer these fundamental questions is to approach them as a sort of marketing problem. Let's start with some ideas held by many young ballplayers:

1. You think you're a fairly talented player, and you would like to be scouted and signed.
2. You think you could make it to the major leagues, because you have those abilities and tools that scouts are looking for.
3. You're eager to capture the scouts' attention now.

But balancing out the marketing equation are factors on the negative side:

1. You're not certain whether your league or team will be scouted.
2. Even if a scout came to watch your team play, you're not sure he'd know who you are.
3. You're deciding which college to attend, and you've always heard that the warm-weather schools attract more scouts to their games.

Let's attack our challenge by addressing those negative factors in the process of getting scouted and signed. In doing so, we'll also deal with some of the myths about the scouting profession.

Will My Team Be Scouted?

We have already discussed various ways that scouts hear about and locate potential prospects. For professional scouts, that process is part of doing a thorough and comprehensive job. Thus, if you play ball for an organized club anywhere in the United States, chances are excellent that the scouts in your area know about your team and will, at some point in the season, come to a game to check out the talent. Some ballplayers, though, don't believe this.

Myth #1: Scouts watch only the bigger high schools and colleges.

This statement couldn't get farther from the truth. All scouts recognize that no school, no matter how big or well-known, has a monopoly on talent. Scouts try to cover every school in their territory during the school year, and in the summer, follow the local summer leagues as well.

Plenty of examples prove this point. California Angels right-hander Willie Fraser, first-round draft choice in 1985, played for tiny Concordia College (New York), where the entire student enrollment is 400. There are few colleges smaller than Concordia, yet scouts flocked to watch Fraser pitch.

Myth #1, though believed by many, just isn't true.

Will the Scouts Know Who I Am?

If you're in a uniform and on the field, the scout will know who you are. He may not know your name and your address, at least not initially. But if you catch his eye, he'll make a mental note to follow up on you.

You don't even have to actually play in a game. A scout attends ball games not primarily to see which team wins or loses, but to find prospects. He may spot an intriguing player taking batting or infield practice even before the game begins. That player may not even be in the game, but the scout will follow up on him.

I like to play a little game with myself as I scout. Particularly if I am going to watch two teams with players that I haven't seen before, I try to get to the field at least an hour before game time. Before I pick up a scorecard or a lineup sheet, I'll observe the players go through their pre-game workouts.

I try to pick out the best prospects on the field just by their movements, actions, and pregame behavior. So if I see a big left-handed first baseman who clouts a couple of long drives during batting practice, I make a mental note to find out his name. Or I might see a wiry little shortstop who seems to gobble up every ground ball hit in his direction. Because I like his range and graceful actions, I will get his name later, too.

The point of my little exercise is to test whether I can indeed spot the best prospects on the field before I've talked with the coaches or gone over the lineups. One reason I play this game is that it sharpens my objectivity on talent.

Scouts are constantly being bombarded by coaches and the media with reports that "this kid is great" or "this guy is a definite first-rounder." By showing up at a ballpark without knowing one player from another, I can be more objective in spotting and gauging talent.

Especially at schools that have outstanding programs, it is during the pregame period that I may spot an impressive underclassman. If I hadn't arrived early to watch the pregame workout, I might not have been aware of this talented sophomore or freshman, because he might not ever get into the game.

It is a reality that, in some programs, talented underclassmen have to sit on the bench and wait until the current starters leave school by signing or graduating. For these younger players, showing off their talents during pregame activities may be vital for their careers.

This discussion leads to another baseball myth:

Myth #2: It's better to be a second-stringer on a nationally recognized team than a starter for a mediocre club.

Though scouts do observe players in pregame warm-ups they always prefer to see players perform in game situations. Thus, in terms of your professional chances, it's better to be with a club for whom you actually *play* than with one that is nationally ranked, but doesn't let you play much.

This applies to both college and summer league teams. The key word is *play*, because ballplayers often wonder whether it's better to be the best player on a relatively weak team or a good player on a relatively good one.

You enhance your chances of being scouted numerous times if you are playing regularly for a good, solid club that has other prospects playing next to you in the lineup. Why? If you're on a team with other talented players looking to get signed, they will attract scouts to your games as well.

Bryan Lambe, a regional scouting supervisor for the Texas Rangers and a former star outfielder in the Detroit Tigers' farm system, makes this point: "If your ballclub happens to have a real blue-chip prospect on it, then you know that all the top scouts in the area are going to be on hand to watch as many games as the prospect plays. And, if you happen to be on that club, and there just happen to be several scouts at every one of your games, well, those scouts are going to have a real good look at that prospect—and at you, too.

"In other words, the better you perform and the better you look, the more opportunity there's going to be to impress the scouts and to catch their eye—even if they really didn't come to see you in the first place."

Lambe makes an excellent point. Although you may not have much choice in what kind of high school or college team you play for, you should for your summer team. If you can hook on with—and start for—a solid summer league club with some very good players, you'll increase your chances of getting noticed by the scouts.

A few summers ago, I went to Warwick, Rhode Island, to scout the American Legion regional tournament. The best teams in the New England area were competing, and I was there to watch a couple of young players who were good, but not really professional prospects.

During one of the games, a young outfielder named Bill Swift came in to pitch a relief stint. The youngster, who was just out of high school, obviously had a strong arm, and he showed he knew something about pitching.

I was impressed and made a note to follow up on Swift. Another observer at the game was obviously impressed with what he saw as well. By the time the game had ended, head coach John Winkin of the University of Maine had offered Swift a baseball scholarship.

The scholarship offer turned out to be a smart move for Winkin. Bill Swift went on to have a great career at Maine, leading the Black Bears to the NCAA World Series in Omaha, and was selected by Seattle as the nation's second overall pick in the 1984 draft. Today, Bill is a member of the Mariner pitching staff. Not too bad for a young outfielder who came in to do a little relief pitching.

The story of Bill Swift gives more evidence to disprove Myth #2. Swift was a good ballplayer, though not necessarily the best, playing on a good American Legion team. When he got the chance to show what he could do on the mound, plenty of scouts and coaches were there to appreciate his abilities.

Of course, if you feel you're good enough as a high school player to become a starter in a top program like the University of Miami or the University of Texas, you ought to apply to those schools. But don't assume that being around a lot of top players will make you a prospect just by association. It doesn't work that way—look back at Brett Butler's odyssey to find the right school (Chapter 5).

There's no question that certain colleges are highly scouted because of their reputation for producing top players. If you're a starter for Miami or Texas, you can rest assured that you'll be seen, simply because many professional scouts attend the Hurricanes' and Longhorns' games.

But your choice of a college should depend on your goals. If you want to attend a school to pursue a high-quality education as well as a baseball career, make your selection based on a variety of criteria, including academics, cost, and location. Make baseball an important part of your decision, but not the overriding factor. There are too many valid considerations beyond the college's baseball program.

The relationship between which college you attend and your chances of receiving a profesional contract is the subject of another baseball fallacy:

Myth #3: You will greatly enhance your chances of getting signed if you play ball in a warm-weather area.

Should I Attend a Warm-Weather College?

In recent years I've heard high school seniors say that if they want to seriously pursue professional baseball, they must attend a college in a warmer part of the country. While there's no question that the climate in the South and Southwest is more conducive to playing baseball, outstanding programs also exist in colder climates.

The scouts know very well that talented baseball prospects are to be found in all parts of the country. And part of the challenge of scouting is discovering talented players in areas of the country that might appear to be inconducive to baseball playing.

Two cold-weather pro players are Dave Winfield and Paul Molitor; both are native Minnesotans who played in the chilly confines of the University of Minnesota ballpark. Pitcher Billy Swift, whose story was told earlier, is from Maine, the country's most northeastern state. In 1986, the New York Yankees drafted Hal Morris, Casey Close, and Scott Kaminiecki from the University of Michigan. Greg McMurtry, the top choice of the Boston Red Sox in the same 1986 draft, was a high school star from Brockton, Massachusetts. And don't forget the Angels' Kirk McCaskill, the hockey-turned-baseball player from the University of Vermont.

All these young men played ball and were scouted in the northern United States. Judging by their success, it would appear that playing in the North did not hurt their chances of being scouted and offered contracts.

The most important aspect of your playing ball is just that—playing ball. To the scouts, it makes little difference whether you're playing in Orono, Maine, or Miami, Florida. What does matter is that you're playing. If you can combine the talent and desire to play pro ball with the opportunity to play regularly and show your skills, the scouts will notice you.

A Few More Myths

Myth #4: Scouts really don't know what they're doing.

Although probably every player who goes unsigned has this thought, there is likely a legitimate reason that he was never offered a contract. This is not to say that scouts don't make mistakes, but in most cases, a clear-cut reason exists when a player is not considered a prospect.

As I have tried to point out, you can be an outstanding high school or college player, with all sorts of records and tributes, and still not qualify as a bona fide professional prospect. By the same token, a particular youngster may have accomplished little during his amateur career, but be looked upon as having terrific professional potential.

Let me illustrate with two disparate examples. Denny Doyle, who played for 10 distinguished years in the major leagues with a number of clubs, including the Boston Red Sox, was a top amateur collegiate player at Morehead State in Kentucky. As a senior, he led his team and its conference in hitting and was subsequently named to several all-star teams.

But when the draft came that June, not one club took a chance on Doyle. Naturally discouraged by this, Denny didn't know exactly what to do. While he was trying to sort out his life's plans, he helped out for a day at a local baseball camp. While he was there, a Red Sox scout asked Denny why he wasn't playing pro ball. When Denny explained he had been bypassed in the draft, the scout gave him an impromptu workout, made a couple of calls, and then offered him a contract. He was on his way.

Contrast Denny's story with that of Cameron Drew, the first-round pick of the Houston Astros in 1985 and considered one of the top prospects in pro ball today.

Cameron came out of the University of New Haven, which is well known by scouts for its baseball programs. But the 6'6'' outfielder originally went to New Haven as a basketball player. Then, one year, Drew thought it might be fun to try out for the baseball team. But he tried out as a pitcher, and on the mound, he was not particularly impressive. As a result, he was cast off to the junior varsity squad. Cameron, realizing that his pitching exploits hadn't impressed head coach Frank "Porky" Vieira, picked up a bat one afternoon and jumped into the batting cage. After he rocked seven or eight shots off the house across the street, way beyond the outfield fence, it was obvious that perhaps Cameron had a future as a hitter. A year later, this previously unheralded basketball player/pitcher had a sensational spring for New Haven varsity baseball, and was "discovered" as a top pick for Houston.

Note the contrast—a top college player goes undrafted but gets a shot at pro ball as a free agent, and a basketball player picks up a baseball bat and becomes an "overnight" star and first-round draft pick. But both got their shot at playing pro ball.

Another baseball myth has to do with pitching:

Myth #5: A pitcher has to throw at least 90 mph to get signed.

The controversies and discussions surrounding a pitcher's velocity are often heated. The average fan seems to think that a scout won't sign an amateur pitcher unless he's another Dwight Gooden. Certainly every scout would like to find the next Dwight Gooden or Roger Clemens, but scouts and baseball front office people are very aware that such talent is an exception.

Let's focus on the importance of velocity, and put it in proper perspective. Tom Seaver—not too bad a pitcher himself—once said that the three skills a pitcher needs to win are movement, location, and velocity. On any given day, he says you can win with two of the three. But if you have only one of the three, you'll lose.

In other words, a pitcher who has great velocity, but no control or movement, is not usually considered a prospect. But, a pitcher who doesn't have great speed but does have outstanding control and movement on the ball, is a prospect. The scouts will follow such a pitcher and sign him.

For an example, consider left-hander Paul Assenmacher of the Atlanta Braves. Paul's typical fastball is clocked between 80 and 84 mph, below the average velocity for major league pitchers. Yet Assenmacher has such a great curveball and slider, plus terrific command of the location of his pitches, that the Braves signed him out of a semipro league in Michigan after he had graduated from Aquinas College.

Was there concern about his lack of velocity when the scouts came around? Says Assenmacher: "Speed can be overrated. You have to mix up your pitches, hit the corners, and throw strikes. Some of the better pitchers in the big leagues don't throw that hard."

Rick Mahler, who won 17 games for Atlanta in 1985, also lacked a blazing fastball and was undrafted. Yet the Braves gave him a chance, and relying upon his control and breaking ball, Rick made it to the major leagues. Braves' scouting director, Paul Snyder, deserves credit for having enough faith in his scouts to allow them to sign pitchers like Assenmacher and Mahler.

So don't be too discouraged if you can't pitch a fastball like Nolan Ryan's. Snyder concludes, "We're all victims of the hard throwers in the major leagues. They catch our eyes, and we'd all like to have one. But there are a lot of guys in the big leagues that throw less-than-85-mph fastballs—especially left-handers."

Art Stewart of the Royals says, "If a young man has an average major league fastball, but it has good life, if it sinks, if he has good location, we'll take a guy like that any day." He means it, too: Royals' pitcher Dan Quisenberry's fastball is consistently clocked in the mid-70s.

What to *Do* to Impress the Scouts

Dress Like a Ballplayer

You've heard about the importance of first impressions. Well, they are important in baseball, too. If you want to be seriously considered as a prospect, always look the part.

Keep your uniform clean; if possible, wash it after every game. Don't "doctor" or customize your uniform, for example, by cutting the stirrups or rolling up the sleeves. Stand out on the field through your play, not your attire.

Does this seem silly? Well, would you go to a job interview dressed in a T-shirt and shorts? Or would you wear an appropriate business suit instead? The same philosophy applies to baseball.

Many times I look at a kid as a possible prospect just because he "looks like a ballplayer." He dresses and carries himself in the way a professional ballplayer would. He's made a positive impression before I've even seen him throw a ball or pick up a bat. Just by his manner he's caught my eye, and I'll be asking the coach about him and his talent.

Hustle on the Field

Scouts go by impressions, and you can control the impressions you make. Showing that you enjoy playing ball by hustling all the time may turn the tide in your favor.

If you were a scout looking at two ballplayers of equal ability, would you be more likely to pursue the youngster who runs to his position on the field and hustles down the baseline or the player who loafs on the field and rarely runs at full speed? That's what scouts mean by hustling—they want to see just how hungry you are to make it.

Be a Team Player

What would you do in the following situation? The score is tied late in the game, and the leadoff man for your club strokes a double. He's the potential go-ahead run, waiting on second base. You're now at bat, with. no outs.

You're a good hitter, and you ask yourself, should I swing away and try for the game-winning hit, or should I try to move the runner along by hitting a grounder to the right side of the field?

As far as the scouts are concerned, the answer is simple. As a team player, you want to move the runner along to third base. That team spirit is what scouts are looking for.

What happens if you decide to swing away, and you get a base hit to win the game? You'll be happy, and celebrate, and probably read about your hit in the paper. But the scouts know that you were selfish and gambled for a hit when instead you should have sacrificed your at bat for the good of the team.

Subtle incidents like this occur in the course of a game or season that indicate your team spirit or the lack thereof. If you're a pitcher, a scout will notice if you become upset when a teammate makes a costly error behind you in a game. He will look to see if you openly root for your teammates when they're up at bat.

Display a Sense of Sportsmanship

It is difficult for a scout to recommend any ballplayer—no matter how great his talent—who instigates a fight on the field or attempts to injure an opponent. That includes such actions as throwing a pitch at a batter, faking a tag so that a runner has to slide at the last moment, or sliding into a base with your spikes high. Tactics like these may seem to you the mark of a "hard-nosed" ballplayer, but as far as scouts are concerned, they label you a troublemaker—and troublemakers don't get signed.

Be Honest and Forthright

If you're fortunate enough to have a professional scout approach you, don't be smug. Answer his questions directly, politely, and honestly. If there is something you don't understand, say so. Honesty still is the best policy.

Demonstrate Your Abilities

A talented kid often assumes that scouts will read about him in the local paper or hear how good he is through the grapevine. Then when a scout finally comes to watch a game, the ballplayer "takes it easy": He doesn't throw at 100% during practice and doesn't run out balls at top speed during the game.

It is a mistake to think that a scout will be impressed enough to sign you based only on what he's read or heard. If you want to get signed, now's the time to show it! Scouts never sign players just because of press clippings or stat sheets. If you have the tools to become a professional player, make certain you show them when the scouts are there.

Smart prospects learn how and when to impress. Let's say you're a shortstop with a great arm. But you have no way of knowing whether you'll get any plays during the game. So, to demonstrate your arm strength, make certain in infield warm-ups that you fire the ball over to first with your best throws.

A catcher or outfielder who has a strong arm should also display it during warm-ups. Or if you have great speed and you pop one up while at bat, hustle down the baseline as fast as you can so the scouts can clock your running speed. Show what you can do! That's the key to making an impression.

What *Not* to Show the Scouts

Certain attitudes and actions will, in general, turn a scout off on your suitability as a professional prospect. Scouts are evaluating not only ballplaying abilities, but also a player's professional attitude toward becoming a major leaguer. That aspect of your appearance and on-the-field presence cannot be overlooked.

Never Act Like a "Hot Dog"

Scouts work at what they do because they love baseball. Some do receive remuneration for their efforts, but, by and large, nobody becomes wealthy being a scout. Because of that love and lifelong admiration for baseball, scouts tend to back off when they see a youngster, particularly a talented one, appear to show off on the playing field. It might be flipping a bat high in the air, or a unique, showy way of catching a fly ball—whatever the action, most scouts are reluctant to recommend a youngster they have come to view as a hot dog.

There certainly are ballplayers who, admittedly, were hot dogs, and still got signed and went on to the majors (Mark Fidrych, who talked to the ball while on the mound, for example). But why run the risk of alienating a scout by showing off?

Avoid Excess in Your Uniform

This is related to the show-off pitfall. Wearing a lucky chain around your neck, or having extra sweatbands on your wrists, or rolling your shirtsleeves up may be important to you. But scouts have little use for the ballplayer who spends excessive time on his wardrobe.

There's nothing wrong with these sorts of ornaments. But you are trying to land a job, and that implies making the best impression you can.

Don't Play if You're Hurt or Coming Off an Injury

There's a difference between playing when you're in pain and playing when you're actually hurt. If you're less than 100% because of an injury, you will only do a disservice to yourself and your team by playing. If you insist on being in the game, and your normal performance is impaired, the scout, who can only go by what he sees you do, will judge you by that.

A scout will not take the time to check before every game he watches whether a player is in good shape. If you're playing in the lineup, he assumes you're ready to be evaluated.

If you're invited to a tryout camp but you are injured, try to be there anyway. That lets the scout know you have the desire, even if you can't play. Tell the scout if you're hurt. If you don't, and you perform poorly, he might write you off.

Don't Disobey Your Coach

Scouts are careful listeners. That's why they hang around the dugouts and around the batting cage before games. They want to learn whether a potential prospect follows his coach well. For example, suppose you're taking batting practice, and your coach yells over to "take two more." The scout watches to see whether you take only two more swings or stay up there so long that the coach is forced to throw you out.

This kind of thing is important to a scout in evaluating a player's coachability. The scout has to determine whether a youngster has the right temperament to accept coaching in the minor leagues. Having the right attitude toward taking orders and instruction is vital in any prospect.

Never "Show Up" an Opposing Player, Coach, or Umpire

Baseball is a game with plenty of frustration—even the best hitters fail 7 out of 10 times at bat! Scouts want to see how you handle adversity, because you will see a lot of it in a pro career. As they watch you, scouts will judge your professional composure, or poise. An amateur ballplayer often allows his game to be destroyed by a bad play in the field, or an umpire missing a close call, or striking out with the bases loaded. He may go into a grandstand act, throwing equipment, or kicking a water cooler, to let everyone in the ballpark know that he thinks he has been wronged.

True professionals, however, have a stronger sense of commitment and poise. They don't like making errors, or getting burned by a bad call, or striking out, but they don't make a public spectacle of it. By and large, they keep their emotions in check, realizing that as professionals, they should take setbacks in stride and be ready for the next pitch or play.

Scouts, as you might expect, are instinctively drawn to a player with professional poise. Nobody particularly enjoys watching an immature display on the field, and no scout wants to reward such actions with a contract.

Don't Be Late for Practice or Getting Onto the Field

Remember that you are selling yourself. If you want the scouts to think you really enjoy playing baseball, show them all you've got during infield and outfield practice and between innings. Sprint out to your position; fire that ball around the field. So few kids do this that you'll be a standout who catches the eyes of the scouts.

Don't Act Tired or Bored

If you give the impression that you're pooped or would rather be doing something else, the scouts will respond to your attitude and write you off. Why bother following a kid who doesn't obviously enjoy playing the game?

Know the Rules!

I'll bet that even though you've followed the game of baseball all your life and have played it for years, you—like thousands of other ball-playing kids—have never read, or even seen, a baseball rule book. Of course you know the obvious stuff, like outs and balls and strikes. But imagine how clever you would appear if you actually studied the rule book and put some of the lesser-known rules into operation. Scouts love seeing a youngster who knows and appreciates the finer points of the game, particularly when they can refer to the rule book for an exact interpretation.

Don't Approach a Scout During a Game
Don't Brag About Yourself to a Scout

There may be occasions when you shouldn't abide by these final two suggestions. But apart from those exceptions, they should be observed.

In general, if you're playing in a game that a scout is watching, refrain from directly approaching him. Scouts cannot afford to be bashful—if one wants to talk to you, he'll find you. And if a scout does speak to you, just answer his questions. Only if he asks should you volunteer your statistics and other achievements.

In a few situations it may be worth your while to ignore the cautions about interacting with scouts. One of the exceptions would be a college senior whom the scouts have not seen play much, as a result of his being injured or platooned or on the bench. Such a player might be looking at his last chance to impress the scouts while in school, and I would say that he has nothing to lose by approaching a scout.

If this is your situation, go up to the scout, introduce yourself, and politely explain why you've decided to approach him. Get right to the point: Tell him you're interested in a pro career, and explain why you think you might have slipped through the cracks.

Don't ask whether he thinks you're a pro prospect; that's too blunt. Keep in mind that scouts are sensitive to pressure from ballplayers and their parents. Just make your explanation and let him respond. If he shows some interest, ask where you can show him your stuff. Perhaps he'll suggest a tryout camp, or say he'll come to a game in which you're definitely going to play. Let him direct the conversation.

Chapter 7

Tryout Camps

Contrary to popular belief, scouts don't stage tryout camps for the purpose of finding prospects and signing them on the spot. Every so often a ballplayer will be offered a contract based upon his showing in a tryout camp, but that is an exception to the rule.

For the most part, a tryout camp allows a scout and his organization to get a close look at some of the better talent in a particular area. Players usually are timed in the 60-yard dash; then outfielders field and throw from the outfield, infielders throw from the infield and field some grounders, and pitchers throw an inning or two. This usually takes place in the morning; in the afternoon, there is likely a game or scrimmage that gives the scouts a chance to see players' reactions and instincts in a game situation.

Since there are 26 major league organizations, you might read about 10 or 12 tryout camps over the course of a year if you live in a major urban area. Each club wants its own scouts to evaluate and judge the talent, so if you're serious about wanting a contract, it is worth your while to attend as many tryout camps as you can. Not only will the experience help you, but the more scouts you impress, the better your chances of being labeled a prospect.

From Amateur to Pro

Every so often someone shows up as an amateur at a tryout camp and by the end of the day is a professional ballplayer. It *is* possible to be signed based upon your performance at a tryout camp. At a Pirates tryout camp some years ago, the Bucs signed a 24-year-old infielder who had finished college and was working as a computer programmer. That "find" was National League slugger Art Howe, who played for several years in the majors. But such signings are extremely rare; you shouldn't expect anything so dramatic at the camps you attend.

It seldom happens that a talented ballplayer shows up at a tryout camp and the scout says to himself, "Hey, where did this guy come from? He's the next Mickey Mantle!" and rushes up to the newly discovered "phenom" with contract and pen in hand. Nine times out of 10, the scout already knows who this prospect is, and he has already planned to offer him a contract. In such cases, the scout is using the camp to take one last look at the ballplayer and to make sure his decision is a good one. This is particularly true when a ballplayer is returning from an injury the season before or has developed a new pitch or type of delivery.

Occasionally, however, a ballplayer comes to a tryout camp and takes the scouts by surprise. Doug Flynn, the former Gold Glove second baseman who has played for the Mets, Expos, Reds, and Tigers, is one of those who showed up at tryout camp and got signed on the spot. Flynn played high school and some college baseball in Kentucky. But Doug, who now stands over 6', was only 5'4" as a high school senior. The scouts noticed him but felt that he would be too small to play ball professionally.

During his college years, Doug preferred basketball and was an outstanding hoop star. It wasn't until he started to grow that he thought about baseball again; even then, he was playing softball rather than baseball. But his friends heard that the Cincinnati Reds were having an open tryout camp and urged Doug to attend. The way Flynn tells the story, he said, yes, he'd go, but on the big day, he overslept. His friends had to roust him out of bed and get him into uniform and over to the camp.

Once there, Doug hit well, fielded flawlessly, showed a strong arm, and displayed excellent speed. As a result, the Reds offered him a contract on the spot. That, however, is an uncommon story. The majority of players at tryout camps are there because the scouts know their talent and want to follow up on them.

Open Versus Closed Tryouts

There are two types of tryout camps—open and closed. The open camps are just that—open to anyone who thinks that he is a potential prospect. An organization may run as many as a dozen of these each year. It typically gets the word out by running an advertisement in the local papers or by telling high school and college coaches. If you have written to a ballclub asking for a tryout, they will notify you about any open tryout camp in your area. (See Appendix B for the *Baseball Blue Book* list of major league baseball organization addresses.)

As you can imagine, such open camps draw hundreds of players, sometimes as many as 500 in one day. The camp usually starts at 9 a.m. and runs all day.

I once ran a camp to which 99 pitchers showed up. Since I wanted each kid to pitch at least one inning in a game situation, the camp lasted until dark. Open tryouts can mean a long day at the ballpark, with a lot of nervous waiting around to show your stuff.

Although you no doubt dream of being offered a contract on the spot, realistically, your purpose for attending a tryout camp is to let the scouts know that you exist, that you have some professional talent, and that they should start a follow-up card on you. If you accomplish those goals, you can consider the camp a success. Most kids who attend tryout camps couldn't sign a contract anyway, because they're still in school. (There are strict rules and regulations covering who can be signed and when. See Appendix A for more information, including selected rules from the *Baseball Blue Book*.)

A closed tryout camp is by invitation only, and only select players are asked to attend. The tryout may be held at a major league stadium; others are staged at local college or high school fields. Wherever they are held, scouts try to keep news of them quiet to avoid attracting crowds.

Scouts usually extend invitations to closed tryout camps through the mail; sometimes a scout will have verbally invited you first. Such camps are normally restricted to between 12 and 30 players; you can assume if you're invited that the scouts are serious about you as a potential prospect.

Normally, the scout will have seen you play several times during the season, or has seen you at an open tryout camp. The closed session is another opportunity to compare you to other top prospects. Occasionally, a scout will invite a ballplayer who's been released by another organization and still wants to play pro ball. Or he may invite a player who looked good last year but suffered a serious injury, to see whether that person can still be considered a prospect. Sometimes a local college coach recommends a senior that he feels has been overlooked by the scouts, and that player may be invited as well.

Closed camps rarely run as long as open camps, simply because there are fewer players present. The activities, however, are the same: You'll be tested on your ability to throw, run, hit, and field. In fact, in the closed camp you're likely to get an even more extensive workout.

The Purpose of Tryout Camps

If you will be attending a tryout camp, set your sights on simply convincing the scouts that you have talent and that they should definitely follow up on you. You are likely to be disappointed if you count on being signed there. The scouts at tryout camps are looking for tools: speed, hitting, throwing, fielding, and power.

You'll be asked to demonstrate your tools; if you are impressive, you will fill out a prospect card listing important information about you. If you get to this step, you deserve congratulations—you have impressed the scouts so well that they want to keep a card on you. That's a significant accomplishment on the road to becoming a professional.

You may wonder how in the world can I make an impression if I'm only allowed a few throws from the outfield or ground balls in the infield? Although it may seem you're not getting much of a shot, remember that the scouts are very experienced in looking for the tools of a major leaguer. They're looking for basic raw material.

A tryout camp is not the setting where a scout attempts to judge your instincts, your ability to play in a game situation, or your desire to win. Rather, it is an opportunity for a scout to check out players' basic baseball abilities.

Your primary aim in this kind of tryout is to impress the scout with your physical abilities. Don't hold anything back—give it your best shot. If the scouts like what they see, they'll be out to watch you play during a regular game.

Remember, too, that at these camps you'll be surrounded by a wide variety of baseball players—skinny, nervous high schoolers who don't know what to expect, seasoned college seniors who are looking to sign, junior college players who want the scouts to notice them. You'll see kids who look terrific and kids who seem to have hardly picked up a baseball before. From the scouts' perspective, tryout camps bring together a great cross-sample of the available talent in your area.

The Open Tryout Camp

Your first activity at camp will be to register your name, age, school, and position on a sheet provided by the scout. You'll probably be asked to sign a form (see Figure 7.1) to agree that you will not hold the major league club or scout responsible if you get injured during the camp. Read the sheet to know what you're signing; but unless you do sign it, you won't be allowed to participate.

Figure 7.1.

Release From Responsibility

The _____ major league baseball club and its affiliates and employees will not be responsible or liable for any injury you may incur during or after the tryout camp.

You are attending this tryout camp at your own risk. Should you receive any type of injury, it will be your own financial responsibility.

You will NOT be allowed to participate in the tryout camp unless you have signed this form (if you are under 21 years of age, your parent or legal guardian must sign). You must present this SIGNED form to our scout or tryout coordinator before entering the tryout camp.

_____

Parent or Guardian

_____   _____

Player   Date

The atmosphere at the start of your tryout camp may be like a carnival or a parade: a carnival because everybody is eager to get the action going, and a parade because of all the different uniforms.

Chances are good that you'll see some friends there. There's nothing wrong with chatting with them before the camp begins or when you're not participating. However, when the head scout speaks to the group, stop talking and pay attention. You don't want to appear disinterested or miss important instructions.

Bring Your Own Equipment!

When you prepare for the tryout camp, imagine that you're going to an all-day job interview. Your uniform should be clean, pressed, and in good condition; your shoes should be shined and well broken in. Bring a jacket, especially if you're a pitcher, and a change of undershirt.

You should also bring along something light to eat, such as a sandwich and a cool drink. Don't assume that the field will have a water fountain, a clubhouse, or a bathrooom. Eat a good-sized breakfast and arrive at the ballpark fully dressed and ready to work out.

In terms of equipment, assume nothing will be provided for you. Bring your own glove (or gloves, if you play different positions) and bat (aluminum is okay, although the scouts may bring wooden ones). If you're a catcher, bring along your own catching equipment. If you can, borrow a batting helmet from your team. Prepare a checklist of equipment, just like a scout does. (Figure 7.2 shows you what the scout brings to a tryout camp.)

The Action

Most open tryout camps are similar in style, but each organization has its own format. Look over the outline in Figure 7.3 (pp. 91–93) for a behind-the-scenes look at the administration of a typical camp. You can gain an edge over the other participants by knowing beforehand what to expect and by practicing the exercises that you'll be asked to perform during the tryout.

Once the administrative matters are taken care of, the ballplayers usually take a lap around the field to get loose. Do some stretching on your own and some calisthenics if you want. Since the first test in the typical camp will be a 60-yard dash, it's important to loosen up and break a sweat.

I would suggest that before your name is called, you get loose and then run a practice 60 yards at full speed. Why? Because you will run a faster

Figure 7.2.

Tryout Camp Equipment Needs

Baseball (use new balls for pitchers and infield drill, used balls for batting)

Catching equipment, including masks, shin guards, chest protectors, etc. (two sets, game and bull pen)

Tryout camp forms

Tryout camp registration cards

Tape measure for 60-yard dash

Stopwatches (2)

Pencils

Clipboards (enough for all workers)

Carbon paper (make enough copies for office and associates)

If you have a ground crew, tip them for their time and assistance.

NOTE: All equipment is available from the home office except for the 60-yard tape measure, clipboards, stopwatches, and pencils. Please purchase any of those items if you need them. Have plenty of pencils for registration.

---

time when your legs are really loose and your body is pumping with adrenaline. Thus, if you run a practice dash, your second one—the one that counts—will show a better time.

Usually the 60-yard dash is run in the outfield, on grass. The scouts mark off the distance and then stage the timings by calling out players' names. You may run by yourself or, if there are many kids to time, you'll run against another player.

If you are running alone, the scout will start timing you when you make your first move. That is, instead of giving you a "ready . . . set . . . go," he'll start the clock as soon as you break from the mark.

Many kids wonder whether it's better to start from a sprinter's crouch or from a base stealer's position, with the legs straddled. I prefer to see a ballplayer start from the base stealing position; after all, that's the kind of start you're going to get in a game. And since you're timed from your first movement, starting like a base stealer as opposed to a sprinter should make little difference in your time.

If you run against another player, the scout normally will give you a "ready . . . set . . . go" so both runners start at the same time. The readings in these races tend to be accurate for the first runner, but less so for the one who comes in second. But don't worry: If the scout wants to see you run again, he'll ask. In most tryout camps, you'll run at least two 60-yarders.

What's a good time? By and large, if you finish in 7.0 seconds or less (7.1 is considered average for a major leaguer), the scouts will take careful note of your name and speed. For more detailed information on the running aspect of the tryout camp, read Figure 7.4 (pp. 93–94). Take note of what the scouts look for, and key your practices to those expectations.

Outfield and Infield Throwing

Once the running is completed, the scouts will most likely test players' outfield and infield arms, or more specifically, arm strength and accuracy. Participants are divided into pairs to throw to each other and loosen their arms up.

The outfielders then are called to center field. At a mark of 250 feet from home, you'll be asked to catch a fly ball, field a grounder, and field a line drive on one hop.

The scouts will watch to see how you approach the ball, how you position your body, how you surround the ball. They'll evaluate your arm strength on your throw to the infield. You may throw to second base or to a cutoff man on the pitcher's mound.

Scouts look for kids who get their bodies under control in the outfield; who have quick arm action and release of the ball, a coordinated throwing action, and accuracy in throwing to a certain spot; and who have a great carry on the ball. By carry, I mean that the throw is strong—it doesn't fade or die away as it approaches the cutoff man.

Remember to catch the ball with two hands and grasp it across the seams. All major league outfielders hold the ball "four seams," which insures that their throws are straight and true and do not sail off the mark. When the ball does bounce, it bounces in a straight line, not off to the side.

Once the outfield action is completed, infielders are placed at shortstop and asked to field three or four grounders and to make throws across to first base. Try to emphasize fundamentals here; keep in mind that the scouts are looking for professional actions. Get your body in front of the ball, keep your backside down, get your arms and hands out in front of your body, plant your back foot solidly, and make a good, hard, on-balance throw to first.

Show quick feet in your infield play. Scouts are looking at you from head to toe, and for infielders—particularly shortstops and second basemen—quick feet are essential. That means being able to adjust your body hurriedly in case of a bad hop or being coordinated enough to move your feet into fielding position on a tough play.

Stay on your toes in the infield and move as fast as you can for the grounders hit your way. Never give the impression that you're plodding along or that you're heavy-footed. Look alert, look quick, and move, move, move!

Once the infielders have finished, the first basemen will be asked to field grounders and throw across the diamond to third. Scouts look for the same kind of skills here: smooth actions, soft hands, quick feet, good range, and an accurate and solid throw. Reread portions of chapter 5 to see precisely what scouts are looking for in a given position.

Catchers are placed behind home and asked to throw out to second base in a simulated stolen-base situation. With a stopwatch, a scout will measure your release time and arm strength (the time of the throw to second base). You'll be given only a few throws, so make certain your arm is loose and ready.

Players With More Than One Position

If you have actually played both outfield and infield recently with your club, then by all means try out at both spots. The same goes if you're a catcher and also play another position. Give the scouts that information on the sign-up sheet. However, if you have played two positions but think that you're much better at one, try out at your better position only.

Pitchers

Most scouts have pitchers throw at least one inning in a game situation. First, though, they will throw on the sidelines while a scout observes. Here, too, the scout is looking for basic tools: velocity, movement, mechanics, breaking pitches, control, and general athletic ability. A scout can tell whether a pitcher has the skills to make it as a professional even without his throwing to a live batter.

Don't be discouraged if you aren't the hardest thrower at the camp. Although any scout would love to find a youngster with a 90-mph fastball, he knows that such pitchers are rare. If your fastball is in the 80s and you have excellent location, great movement on the ball, or an outstanding breaking pitch, a scout will certainly take note of you.

On the sidelines you will only throw 20 to 25 pitches, so don't hold back. Although you'll be tempted, don't overthrow either. Make certain you can control what you throw.

To the Game!

If there is enough time after the testing is completed, the scouts will hold a quick round of infield/outfield practice. If this happens, go to the position where you feel most comfortable.

Try to show plenty of spark. Make noise. Whistle. You're competing against all the players there to capture the scouts' attention. If you're good at making chatter, that's another way to let the scouts know you're a ballplayer worth watching.

In a simulated game, two teams will be put together haphazardly, and a parade of pitchers will throw one inning (six outs) each. There is little rhyme or reason to how the teams are drawn up, so don't worry about what team you're on or where you bat in the order. In fact, the batting order may just go round the defensive lineup; that is, the catcher hits first, then the first baseman, the second basemen, and so on.

If you're not selected to play in the first lineup, find a place off the field in the shade and relax as best you can. The action usually goes fairly quickly, and as each batter gets his turn (usually two at bats), he is replaced by someone waiting for his turn. The scouts make sure that everybody gets a chance to show his stuff.

You may be tempted during these lulls in the action to sit back, eat some lunch, even read the newspaper. You may wait for quite some time, but try not to give the impression that baseball isn't uppermost in your mind. Be ready whenever your name is called.

A Word About Hitting

When your turn comes to bat, hit the ball hard and run as fast as you can to first. Don't make hitting complicated. Get a strike you can handle and go to work on it. Don't swing at poor pitches. Even if the pitcher can't find the strike zone, don't feel rushed. This is your chance to show what you can do.

There usually are not umpires at tryout camps, so the catchers call balls and strikes to keep things moving along. Keep in mind that if you swing at bad pitches, the scout can only assume that you don't know where the strike zone is.

In watching you bat, the scout is not as interested in whether you get a base hit or fly out as he is in analyzing your swing. Do you have quick hands? Is your bat speed good? Are you keeping your hands back? What about your balance?

Remember that scouts want to see the ball jump off your bat. There are base hits and there are *base hits*. The kids who really smack the ball hard are the ones who will be looked at as the real prospects. The scouts would rather see two bullet-like groundouts than a flare or soft liner that falls in for a hit.

The outcome of your at bats will not necessarily determine how you are viewed as a prospect. Scouts do not assume that the youngster who hits well in a tryout is a more likely prospect than one who strikes out. After all, the kid who fans twice might be only 17 years old and batting against a top college pitcher who's 22. If he has been noticed because he's a terrific middle infielder, his hitting isn't as important as his defensive tools.

By the same token, a youngster might lash two line-drive hits in the tryout. But the scouts view him as an outfielder who hits line drives rather than home runs and who, unfortunately, doesn't run particularly well. He may be a good hitter, but in terms of an optimal skill combination or the professional "blueprint" scouts rely on, an outfielder who has only average speed and little power isn't likely to fit the ballclub's needs.

That blueprint for signability, often overlooked by young ballplayers, helps explain why scouts pass on some players. For example, until LaSchelle Tarver was traded by the Mets to the Red Sox in 1985, he was a talented player caught in the wrong blueprint. LaSchelle had always been a top hitter in the minors, including a .326 year at Tidewater in 1984 and .311 in 1985. The problem? Where LaSchelle could play defensively.

Most major league clubs want their left and right fielders to be power hitters, able to club 20 or more homers a year. The center fielder is usually speedy—a guy who doesn't hit many homers but can steal 50 bases in a season. Tarver rarely hit more than a few homers in a season and unfortunately, never stole many bases either. As a result, he didn't fit into the typical ballclub's blueprint for outfielders.

But LaSchelle got a break when he was traded from the National League Mets to the American League Boston Red Sox. It seems that the designated hitter was a position that LaSchelle fit nicely.

After the Tryout Is Over . . .

At the end of the day, the head scout will undoubtedly gather the players and thank everyone for coming. He might make general comments about everybody's hard work and the talent he saw on the playing field, but don't expect a specific critique of your game. It's not that the scout doesn't care or want to give positive feedback, but it wouldn't be fair to single out one or two players.

Once the tryout has ended, pack up your things and head on home. Don't wait around to talk to the scout unless he specifically asks you to.

Remember that scouts use tryout camps to bring in talented ballplayers and see how they've developed over the year and how they compare with other players. As a result, don't expect an immediate call or letter from a scout after a tryout. If he doesn't contact you, wait until the next tryout and repeat your efforts. If you have the tools and attitude that scouts are looking for in professional prospects, you'll make your impression.

A Quick Review

When the tryout day comes:

- Arrive at the field on time, or even a little early. You're not likely to make a good impression if you are late.
- Bring your own equipment: spikes, gloves, bats, catching equipment, even batting helmet. Don't assume anything—bring it all.
- Make certain you're loose. Warm up and then stretch before you start to work out hard. If you've been injured, make sure you tell the scout in charge.
- Wear a sharp, clean uniform. Scouts will form an instant impression based on your appearance.
- Bring a small lunch and something to drink. You are likely to be at the field all day, and will probably be warm. Don't assume that there will be a functioning water fountain at the field.
- Hustle. Scouts want to know whether you really want to ''play the game.'' Show them you do by hustling all the time.

Figure 7.3.

Conducting the Tryout

1. Assemble participants on the grass, facing away from the sun. The person in charge makes a few introductory remarks, telling the purpose of the camp and what will happen. Describe the procedure to be used so the players will know what to expect, e.g., warm-up exercises and jogging followed by catch, pepper, infield and outfield, pitchers' procedures.
2. Have ballplayers line up according to position played, one behind another, with the low number in front as shown on the following chart.

| | | | Position | | | |
	3B	SS	2B	1B	C	OF	P
Player	3	6	16	11	9	29	20
Number	1	4	12	10	5	27	20

Enter numbers on player evaluation sheets. Be sure each player knows his number.
3. Ask whether any participant has an injury, sore arm, blisters, or other condition you should know about. Have those players raise their hands, then talk with each individually (don't make them announce their maladies to the whole group).
4. Perform warm-up exercises. Caution the group not to wear themselves out warming up!

   a. Jog around the field.
   b. Do stretching and flexibility exercises.

5. Divide into groups of five or six and play pepper. Pitchers and catchers pair off and warm up.
6. Send pitchers and catchers to bull pen. Scout or designated coach rates pitchers on fastball, curve, etc. Circle the numbers of pitchers who perform best. They will be first to pitch in batting practice. Use radar gun. Be specific.
7. Have remaining players line up in two rows facing each other, 90 feet apart, pair off, and play catch. Tell them to throw overhand and aim chest-high. Scout circulates among players, observing form and arm action, and making appropriate notations on evaluation sheet. Stress playing catch properly (feet, rhythm, constant flex, etc.).

(Cont.)

Figure 7.3 (Cont.)

8. Outfielders line up in center field and throw to third base and home. Third baseman and catcher are in position to receive throws. Shortstop positions himself in line with center fielder and third base, arms raised, facing center field. He should not cut off throws, however. Each outfielder makes about five throws, then goes to right field and makes two throws to third, ball hit at the outfielder—then scout should fungo ball down right field line, make outfielder go to the line and throw home.

9. While outfielders are being evaluated, infielders warm up playing pepper.

10. Infielders take their respective positions and scout hits infield. Hit to all positions so the players keep active. Emphasize long throws. Arms are graded best by observing long throws. Use a stopwatch to get times on catchers' throws to second base.

11. After infielders and outfielders have thrown, move all players to 60-yard dash course.

12. Give brief clinic on form running, stressing proper sprinting technique. The course should be laid out along a foul line or other suitable reference line (otherwise, players do not run in a straight line and times are inaccurate). Try to avoid running either with or against the wind; i.e., run at a right angle to the wind.

13. Candidates should run in pairs. Starting position is as in leading off first base (crossover step). Right foot is on the starting line. Pitchers and catchers run first. When they are finished, send in pairs to warm up in the bull pen for batting practice while the rest of the position players run the dash.

    Average major league time for 60 yards using the crossover step start is 7.1 seconds.

    NOTE: Have timers start watch on respective runner's initial movement. The timer must force himself to wait until the runner *hits* the finish line and then stop the watch as fast as he can. By not anticipating the runner, the initial lag is cancelled out and the time will be accurate.

14. Call position players in five at a time and begin batting practice. Make sure to designate ball shaggers and two pitchers on the ball bucket, behind second base, to keep the bucket on mound full at all times. Have hitter bunt first two pitches—down the

(Cont.)

Figure 7.3 (Cont.)

third-base and first-base lines. Next pitch, hit and run; next pitch, move runner from second to third with one out. Then five swings and out—move on to next hitter.

Each batting practice pitcher should throw out approximately three hitters, with scout using radar gun to record speed. Scout should be situated behind cage to grade pitchers, as well as to instruct them about which pitch to throw, etc. This also enables scout to make sure BP routine is being followed by hitters, and enables scout to grade hitters.

Figure 7.4.

Running Times and Clocking Players

Our organization believes that *SPEED is a vital aspect of a position player's abilities* and plays a very important part in the success of a team and a ballclub. Whenever you evaluate a first and a second division club in any league or a successful ballclub with an unsuccessful one, speed plays a prominent role.

Second division clubs are usually handicapped by a lack of speed. Speed plays a very important part not only in the offensive output of a club but also in its defense, particularly in the outfield.

The measurement of actual running speed varies among players and can be very deceptive. For example, a short person usually takes more steps getting to where he wants to go and therefore may give an illusion of a certain level of speed. In actuality, he may only be a fair runner, because he is taking a lot more steps.

On the other hand, the tall guy with long legs and long strides may not look as fast, but may get where he wants to go quicker. To remove any guesswork we put the evaluation of speed on a very technical basis. *Therefore, every player must be timed with a stopwatch.*

Policy

All Players for Draft

60-yd Dash

50	6.9–7.0	Average
60	6.8–6.7	Above average
70	6.6–6.5	Good
80	6.4	Outstanding

(Cont.)

Figure 7.4 (Cont.)

Procedure for Clocking Players

Start the clock as soon as the batter makes contact with the ball. You should not wait until contact has been made, but rather let your instinct direct you as to exactly when to start the stopwatch. In other words, it is an instinctive anticipation; as the ball arrives in the hitting zone you will instinctively start the clock. You stop the clock when the batter's foot touches first base.

Listed below is a breakdown of running times and how they fit into the numerical grade of speed. (This scale is used by the Major League Scouting Bureau and a number of other organizations.)

From right side	From left side
4.6 – 2	4.5 – 2
4.5 – 3	4.4 – 3
4.4 – 4	4.3 – 4
4.3 – 5	4.2 – 5
4.2 – 6	4.1 – 6
4.1 – 7	4.0 – 7
4.0 – 8	3.9 – 8

Be prepared to clock every runner every time he comes to bat, and record the actual running times on all reports. In addition, list your evaluation of his running speed.

It is possible to see an entire game without getting a true running time on a particular player because he never hits a ball that demands running at full speed. However, you are still to clock all players and record their times. Failure to run out a ball may be an indication of a player's lack of hustle, desire, and makeup. This should be noted.

Chapter 8

The Tools
and Terms
of the Trade

You will have better insight into what kinds of talents a scout looks for by learning the tools and terms he uses when he scans a ball game. In this chapter, the major components of the scout's trade are described and their functions explained.

The Scout's Manual: Club Philosophy for Success

In most ballclubs, the first things a new scout is given are not a folding chair and a straw hat, but the club's scouting manual and an indoctrination into the team's philosophy or blueprint for finding championship major league talent. Before that scout is unleashed to scour a territory for talented young players, he needs to know what he's looking for—or more to the point, what the club's front office is looking for.

There are substantial differences among team blueprints; they are well illustrated by the differences you can observe among the 26 major league clubs. For example, the Yankees traditionally bolster their lineup with long-ball, and preferably left-side, hitters. The Kansas City Royals and Los Angeles Dodgers prefer to build championship teams with power pitchers. And the St. Louis Cardinals think they can win with exceptional team speed, particularly if the batters can switch-hit.

The top management of each club puts together a composite of what they want, or need, at each position. This "dream team," determined by a variety of factors, is a reflection of the management's philosophy for a pennant-winning ballclub.

Details of this composite are integrated into the club's scouting manual, so that each scout has a solid idea of the types of prospects to look for. Thus, when I scout a ballplayer, I evaluate him in light of what my organization wants in a prospect. Not every talented player can necessarily meet our needs.

A high school or college player might be considered a terrific prospect by one scout, but not one at all by a scout from a different club. You've probably wondered why some teams follow a certain prospect while others show no interest. Their blueprints are often the reason.

As I scout players it's not enough for me merely to think that a certain young man is a potential professional. I must believe that he has potential not only to make it to the major leagues, but also to win there. That may sound demanding, but as a business, the goal of major league baseball teams is to win the World Series.

As you might suspect, most clubs keep their scouting manuals and blueprints for success top secret. Don't expect a scout to tell you or your coach what those plans are, nor should you ask. Figure 8.1 lists just some of the forms that make up a traditional manual.

By now it should be apparent that filling out and maintaining forms is a large part of a scout's job. But it might surprise you that a scout has to keep up with the paperwork even after a prospect is "signed, sealed, and delivered" to the professional ballclub.

Figure 8.1.

Scouts' Information Forms

- Form letter for schedule and roster request
- Prospect information cards
- Daily-game work cards
- Cross-check work pad
- Incentive bonus plan
- Contract tender letter
- Signed player questionnaire
- Player strength and weakness form
- Scouting credits on signed players
- Professional club reports
- Free agent report form
- Free agent follow-up report form
- Non-pro club report
- Professional individual reports
- Cross-check report form
- Professional preferential list
- Secondary phase final summary sheet
- Regular phase final summary sheet
- Final draft cards
- Tryout camp registration cards
- Tryout camp worksheet (pitchers)
- Tryout camp worksheet (players)
- Tryout camp release-from-responsibility letter
- Tryout camp permission letter allowing youngster to participate
- Prospect information form
- Health history
- Signability questionnaire
- Uniform player contracts
- Consent to re-select
- College scholarship plan
- Information request letter

Figure 8.2.

Signed Player's Outline

This form is to be prepared by the scout and mailed to the home office along with player contract, or soon thereafter.

Part A

- Player's name
- Position
- Address (city, state, zip code)
- Home telephone (area code)
- Date of birth

- Bats
- Throws
- Glasses/contacts?
- Race

Part B

- If switch-hitter, hits better from _____

- If present position is best chance to succeed in pro ball, state why:

  _____

  _____

- If present position is not best chance to succeed in pro ball, then state what position you recommend and why:

  _____

  _____

- How many games have you seen him play to date?

  High School   College

  American Legion   Others

- State any injury, illness, or physical ailments that may handicap or affect his full potential. List each item and date of injury:

  _____

  _____

- Scout's evaluation of above:

  _____

  _____

Figure 8.3.

Player's Publicity Questionnaire

This form to be returned with player's contract.

Name _____

Nickname _____

Position _____ Nationality _____

Home address _____
                 city   state   zip

Telephone _(   ) _____

Place of birth _____
              city   state

Date of birth _____
             month   day   year

Height _____ Weight _____ Hair color _____ Eye color _____

Bat _____ Throw _____

Club with which you signed your first professional baseball contract

_____
Club   scout who signed you   date

Circumstances leading to your first contract offer _____

_____

High school attended _____
                                             city   state

_____
year graduated   sports you played

High school athletic achievements _____

_____

College attended _____
                                       city   state

_____
year graduated   degrees

(Cont.)

Figure 8.3. (Cont.)

College sports (achievements) _____

_____

Is there anyone to whom you particularly owe your success in baseball? Why?

_____

Who is your baseball hero? Why? _____

_____

Did you play on the same club or in the same league with players now prominent in the major leagues? (club, league, players) _____

_____

Tell about your greatest thrill in baseball _____

_____

Championship teams on which you have played

_____
team name   year

Most difficult thing to do in baseball _____

_____

Hobbies _____

_____

Winter occupation _____

Personal superstitions _____

_____

Marital status (wife's name/date of marriage, names/birthdates of children)

_____

_____

Original baseball position (If position has changed, why? When? By whom?)

_____

_____

Once a contract is signed, a scout has to fill out more forms, like the two in Figures 8.2 and 8.3. Suppose you had to fill the "Signed Player's Outline" on yourself. How would you judge a question like best position? If a scout handed you the "Player's Publicity Questionnaire," could you make it impressive and interesting? Personal public relations will become part of the game once you've signed. Questions like your greatest thrill or your most difficult achievement could be grist for media coverage for yourself even now.

A Scout's Notebook—His Bible

Once a scout has a firm sense of what he will be looking for in prospects, he puts together a notebook. That book, which he takes to every game he scouts, contains all the basic and vital information on each player.

In my notebook, I record two sets of information on each player. First are the basic data: height, weight, bats right or left, throws right or left, date of birth, education and current position. Second are my scouting observations. Does this youngster fit my club's blueprint? To answer that question I have to take note of each young man's physical and psychological tools.

I look at the ballplayer from every perspective. What kind of natural athletic ability does he have? Is he going to grow much taller? Is he likely to put on weight as he matures? Is his body flexible? Does he have the drive to improve? How does he handle adversity on the field? What kind of rapport does he have with his teammates and his coach? How about the umpires, and even the other team? These questions, and many more, have to be asked—and answered.

The Famous—or Infamous—Radar Gun

The portable radar gun was introduced to professional baseball on a wide scale in the 1970s. Some say that it has revolutionized the profession of scouting, that it has made an art more of a science, especially in evaluating pitchers.

Others feel just as strongly that a radar gun, if used improperly, can do as much damage as good for scouting.

The controversy rages on. Certainly, any baseball fan loves to see the gun register in the high 90s for a Dwight Gooden or a Nolan Ryan. For the one-in-a-million kid who can fire that high, hard one, the radar gun can instantly confirm a scout's greatest hope—that he really has discovered the next Gooden or Ryan.

I view the radar gun as just another scouting tool. I like it and I use it. But I make certain I don't get carried away with its influence. The gun measures only one thing—speed. Pure, raw speed. Nothing more. And there's a lot more to a successful pitching prospect than just speed.

For example, the gun does not measure the ball's movement, or the sharpness of a curve or a slider, or the pitch's location on the plate. All it does is measure speed, and speed alone cannot guarantee a contract. For every Dwight Gooden or Roger Clemens in the majors, there are dozens of unknown pitchers in the low minors who can throw just as hard but never conquer the finer points of pitching.

Pitching coaches on the major league level will tell you that to be a winner, a pitcher must have movement on the ball. It's always more difficult for a batter to make contact with a pitch that comes in at, say, 88 mph but sinks down or shoots away than to hit a 94-mph fastball that is as straight as an arrow.

Why? Simple physics. A batter has greater eye-to-hand motor control with a pitch that comes in a straight line, no matter how fast it comes. He might swing a little late or foul the ball back, but an experienced hitter will adjust for the increased speed, choke up a little on the bat, and then hit the next straight fastball right on the money.

In contrast, the ball that comes in slower but has great—and unpredictable—movement is more difficult to hit, because the movement adds a new variable to the eye-to-hand control required. Not only must the batter cope with the velocity of the pitch, he must also track the ball's movement to make contact. And there's no predictibility to the pitches—one may sink down while the next one moves away.

It's easier to hit a ball that's always going to be in the same place, regardless of the ball's speed, than it is to hit a pitch that's always moving. This is obvious to most followers of baseball, but it bears repeating when it comes to radar guns.

It's well accepted in scouting circles that different guns are calibrated in different ways. As a result, one radar gun may clock a pitch at 90 mph while a different gun measures the same pitch at 86 or 87 mph.

A few miles per hour may not seem like a big difference, but in scouting a pitching prospect, 3-4 mph might determine whether a contract is offered. So you can see that the accuracy of a radar gun is crucial.

I feel that the use of the radar gun has been great for baseball and for scouting. It adds precision, and I have found it particularly helpful in clocking pitchers at night or in a gym; when watching a pitcher under artificial light, the user's perception of a pitch's velocity can be thrown off. The radar gun gives a scout a relative standard of how hard a young man is throwing.

Sometimes a radar gun will flash two speeds. One speed appears on the screen then quickly disappears to be replaced by a second reading. In a case like this the radar gun has recorded two speeds. The first number is the speed of the ball as it leaves the pitcher's hand. The second number, which most scouts refer to, is the maximum velocity the ball reaches on its flight to the plate. That maximum speed might occur when the ball is halfway to the plate, three-quarters of the way there, or even as it crosses the plate. Most physics experts agree that the pitch reaches a top speed and then actually slows down a bit by the time it reaches the batter.

I have mentioned that I look upon the radar gun as just another part of my scouting repertoire. In recent years, I have used the gun to measure not only pitching velocity, but the relative strength of outfielders and infielders. How better to find out just how strong a fielder's arm is than by clocking a throw with a radar gun? Here again, though, the gun can measure speed, and nothing more. A shortstop might have a tremendously strong arm, but if he can't throw accurately across the diamond, he won't be considered a prospect. The scout still must determine the many factors beyond speed.

The Scout's Stopwatch

Every scout carries a stopwatch. Like a radar gun, a stopwatch measures raw speed, and for that it is invaluable. But just as a radar gun cannot measure a pitch's movement or location, a stopwatch cannot measure what kind of jump a base stealer gets on a pitcher or what kinds of instincts a runner has on the base paths.

Nonetheless, determining a player's speed is essential. Raw speed is one of those tools that really cannot be taught, although you may be able to improve your speed through diligent exercise (see chapter 5). Scouts love to see a young man with speed to burn. Players like Rickey Henderson, Vince Coleman, and John Cangelosi have shown that leg speed can really break a game open offensively.

Timing Base Running and Fielding

Scouts time each batter when he comes to the plate. Clocking a player's run from home to first gives the scout a fairly good idea of how fast he is. Scouts have developed a standard scale for a home-to-first run: the major league average for a right-handed batter (clocked from the time the bat makes contact with the ball) is 4.3 seconds. For left-handed hitters, the average is 4.2 seconds.

Those numbers can give you a goal to work toward. Get a stopwatch and have a coach, a parent, or a friend time you. Remember that the clock should be started not when you swing the bat but when you hit the ball.

Speed plays a major role in baseball. Most casual fans think of speed only in connection with stealing a base. But speed has many different applications. How many times have you seen a quick-legged center fielder like Gary Pettis or Brett Butler race down a well-hit fly ball and turn a "sure" double into a long out? That's speed at work.

The speed of a lead-off hitter like Dave Collins influences the play of a game. Because Dave runs so well, the infielders have to play a little closer to the plate than usual. The defensive players also know that on a close play, such as a ground ball in the hole or a bunt, they will have to rush their throws a bit because of Collins' speed. Rushing a play, of course, dramatically increases the chances for a mistake or fielding error. Again, the ability to run makes the difference.

There are many other illustrations of the importance of speed in baseball. A fleet-footed outfielder can hold a ball in the gap to a long single instead of a double if he is fast enough to cut the ball off. A fast base runner can take the extra base—instead of stopping at second he can chance going on to third. A hitter who runs well can prevent a double play by getting down the line to first.

If you are being scouted in a game, make certain you run out every fly ball, grounder, hit—*everything*—to first base as hard and as fast as you can.

Why? Because a scout can only judge what you do, not what you say: that point cannot be overemphasized. You may be quick on your feet, but unless you show me you can really scoot, I won't mark it down on my notebook. If speed is one of your assets, be aggressive: show me you can run. Once is all it will take to get my attention.

Some scouts like to time runners from first to third. Others prefer to get a reading on how long it takes you to run the bases at top speed. A scout might also use that exercise to see if you know how to cut a base or how to hit the bag with your foot and then push off for greater acceleration.

Putting Catchers on the Clock

Stopwatches are also used to clock a catcher's throw to second base. Major league scouts know that unless a catcher can catch a pitch and make the throw to second in 1.8 or 2.0 seconds, he will have difficulty throwing out professional base stealers.

Here's the breakdown: The stopwatch starts at the instant the catcher receives the pitch. It is stopped just as the ball reaches second. The throw has to be accurate—right on the money.

This timing is essential, because some catchers have terrifically strong arms but take too much time getting the ball out of their gloves and making their throws. At the other end of the spectrum might be a player whose arm is only so-so, but who gets rid of the ball in a hurry. The clock tells the scout just how a particular catcher might fare against a talented runner.

Scouts realize that most base runners steal on the pitcher, not the catcher. To compensate for that, a scout will time the entire battery; that is, he'll start his stopwatch when the pitcher comes out of his stretch and makes the pitch to home. The clock stops once the ball reaches second base, after the catcher has fired the ball down there. The total time a scout accepts for all this is 3.3–3.5 seconds. Why? Because the typical base stealer in the major leagues takes that long to get from first to second on an attempted steal.

There are other variables involved in base stealing. Some pitchers throw harder than others. A fastball coming in at 90 mph gets to the catcher a lot faster than a slow curve at 75 mph. That's one reason it's better to try to steal on a curveball pitcher than on a hard thrower.

Although the typical base stealer needs approximately 3.5 seconds to go from first to second, some guys, like the Yankees' Rickey Henderson or Eric Davis of the Reds, are consistently clocked at 3.3 seconds. That may not seem like a subtantial difference. But it's only 90 feet—30 yards—between first and second, and .2 seconds can make a dramatic difference when you need that stolen base.

The Follow-Up File

Each scout has a system for keeping files on prospects; next to my scouting notebook, those files are my most treasured possession.

I have described how I gather lineups and make individualized notes on each player who participates in a game I observe as a scout. That evening I go over the day's notes. I review the observations I've made, and make any other notations that come to mind. Figure 8.4 shows some typical comments.

For example, I might have seen a talented center fielder whose speed impressed me. But he's only a sophomore in high school, and not eligible

Figure 8.4.

Follow-Up Report

Why this player should be followed:

Player 1.

Average build, average body. Smooth, efficient, quick catching actions; quick release with average arm and accuracy when needed; heady receiver, handler of pitches.

Lacks strength at present to hit long ball; rakes at ball; body and size indicate limited stamina and durability.

Watch closely for development, especially strength through maturity.

Player 2.

Tall, raw-boned, good pitcher's body; average major league velocity with loose arm. Does not use mound well for leverage, dead front side. No pull, rushes; potential tremendous mechanical adjustment. Little deception in delivery; fastball straight. Hits lot of bats, but with playing time, pro improvement and instruction can take off.

Watch closely for improvement. Possible transfer to other school.

Player 3.

No known injuries, medium build, compact, strong; loose, live, rubber-armed reliever; low 3/4; fastball sinks, tails well; curveball deceptive; hides ball.

Fastball lacks major league velocity. Curveball not tight. Only merits watching to see if fastball improves.

to be signed. I write his name, position, high school, and so on, on a follow-up card and file it away. Since this youngster has two more years of high school, I would file him in my card deck for next spring.

Or I might have seen a third baseman with quickness and range but only an average arm. He's a senior with some hitting tools and, judging from my notes, might be a sleeper of a prospect—not as a third baseman but rather at second. Again, I file all his vital information on a follow-up card.

However, since this player is a senior and eligible for the free agent draft, I place his card in my special follow-up file for this year. I review that file weekly because I must go back and watch the youngsters in it soon, before the draft. Then if I still think a certain player is a prospect, I will contact a cross-checker to come see him play.

As you can imagine, my filing system becomes quite crowded by the end of the school year, after I have seen hundreds of high school, junior college, and college games. Not only do I keep each game on record, but I also write up a card on every ballplayer who catches my eye.

Although this is my own system for keeping track of hundreds of prospects I see, each scout undoubtedly develops his own.

You can see why it's so important that you show your skills when a scout is watching. A tip-off to your abilities through a newspaper story or from a coach or even an umpire probably brought him to your game. But from that point on, you have to show your stuff.

If you have outstanding speed, show it. If you have a great arm from the outfield, make certain you show it during practice and, if the chance arises, during the game. If you have a masterful curveball, make sure you throw it—and throw it for strikes. My point is simple: Just show me once that you can hit a ball 450 feet, or that you can run to first in less than four seconds, or that you can throw a pitch 90 mph, and believe me, your name will be on the follow-up list.

And once you're on that list, you're guaranteed that I'll be back to see you again. And that's the first step on the road to getting signed.

Chapter 9

Extra Innings: Common Questions Answered

In my years of playing, coaching, and scouting in professional baseball, I've heard probably every question you could imagine from prospects. I have given many of the answers in previous chapters. However, to tie up any loose ends, I want to address some of the most common questions I hear from ballplayers.

Question: Are there particular programs in which a high school senior or junior college player can make himself known to college coaches and pro scouts?

For years, most college coaches and, to a lesser degree, pro scouts have relied upon networks of contacts. Coaches, having to recruit new players each year, call upon colleagues, high school and American Legion coaches, local sportswriters, alumni, and anyone else they think may be able to recommend an outstanding high school player.

Once a potential player has been identified, the coach normally dispatches an assistant coach to watch the youngster play. If the assistant feels that the youngster is good enough, the head coach will come to watch him play and perhaps will offer him a scholarship.

As you can imagine, such a system of contacts and follow-up can be haphazard. In fact, most college coaches would tell you that recruiting talented players depends mostly on luck—being in the right place at the right time. It is ironic that although championship college ballclubs are built upon talented players, there isn't a very systematic way of letting those coaches know about good high school players.

Question: What if I just get myself into shape and go to some spring-training sites in Florida and Arizona: Will the pros give me a tryout down there?

In most cases, if you just show up at a spring-training site and ask for a tryout, you'll be turned away. At best, you'll be told about the next open tryout camp in or near your hometown.

Occasionally a few clubs, like the St. Louis Cardinals and the Kansas City Royals, stage open tryouts for one morning during spring training. On that morning anyone can come and try out in front of the scouts. To learn the dates and locations of these tryouts write to these clubs during the winter months and ask.

Question: How about if I go directly to a Class A or AA club and ask the manager for a tryout?

You'll probably run into the same kind of closed door as you would in spring training. Unless you're a former minor leaguer who already has a release, the manager will probably tell you that he's sorry, but due to the insurance risks or major league club policy, he can't allow you to try out.

I'm certain that on rare occasions someone has asked for a tryout and been given one and even has signed, but the odds of that happening are extremely low. For better or worse, minor league clubs tend to insulate themselves from "walk-ons."

If you have played pro ball before, the manager will most likely call his front office and ask for a computer printout on you and your abilities from the club's scouting system. If the report is negative or lukewarm, you'll probably be told thanks, but no thanks. However, if the report is a good one, you might be allowed to try out.

Question: If I contact the major league clubs personally, will they send a scout to see me play?

First of all, if you do contact a major league club, make certain you write rather than call. Most scouts work out of their homes, so a phone call to the club's front office will probably dead-end. But ballclubs are good at corresponding by mail, so your chances of getting a response are better if you write.

Be sure to enclose a stamped return envelope with your home address with your inquiry. In your letter, ask when and where they plan to hold a tryout camp in your area. If you decide to send some clippings of your best games, a half dozen or fewer should get your point across.

At this juncture, information is all you can reasonably request of the ballclub. But by taking the time to write, you should hear in a few weeks about as many as 12 to 16 tryout camps, all of which you'll be invited to attend.

Question: Where do I get names and addresses for the clubs?

For a complete listing of all 26 major league clubs and addresses, turn to Appendix B.

Question: What is the difference between a "co-op" team and an "independent" club in the minors?

A co-op, or cooperative team is a professional ballclub that has on its roster ballplayers whose contracts are owned by major league ballclubs. Say the Appalachian League has a co-op team playing in Bristol, Virginia. On that ballclub, you might find five players whose contracts belong to the Detroit Tigers, seven players owned by the St. Louis Cardinals, and 10 who are part of the New York Mets club.

The reason they are all thrown together in one club is that their own ballclubs don't have enough roster spaces on other minor league affiliates for them to play there. Rather than having such players idle or releasing them, the various front offices have placed them on a co-op team.

Most major league clubs would prefer to have all their kids play on the club's own minor league teams. But if a system is overstocked with players, a co-op is a very logical and convenient solution, allowing these 20 or so players a chance to play pro ball on a daily basis.

In contrast to a co-op, an independent club is made up of ballplayers who do not have contracts with any of the major league teams. Instead, their contracts are with the individual owner of the independent club, and each ballplayer is employed by and paid by that owner.

Every season there are a few independent clubs, usually Class A, around the country. Recently, the most famous have been the Miami Marlins of the Florida State League, the Utica Blue Sox of the New York-Penn League, and the San Jose Bees of the California League. You've probably heard about former major leaguers who have signed on with these clubs in hopes of reattracting another major league contract.

If you feel that you've been overlooked by the major league scouts, and you still want to play pro ball, signing with an independent club will give you all the experiences of playing minor league ball. But keep in mind that an independent club is nothing more than a showcase for your talents—a good year there doesn't guarantee that you'll be signed by a major league club.

If you belong to, say, the Pittsburgh Pirates and have an excellent year in Class A ball, there's every expectation that you'll be moved to Class AA the next spring. But with an independent club, there's really no progression or ladder to climb. It's just one club in one league with one owner.

On the bright side, you are playing ball in a professional setting, and occasionally a player from an independent club will be seen, scouted, and signed by one of the major league clubs. But, once again, this is more the exception than the rule, and scouts know it.

But you never know what might happen once you're in a professional arena. A few years ago, when I was coaching in the Atlantic Collegiate Baseball League, our team had a bright, affable left-hander named Rob Nelson who was a top-notch pitcher at Cornell. Like everybody else, he was looking to get signed.

Unfortunately, Nelson never got drafted. But he decided he wanted to play pro ball and hooked up with an independent team in Portland, Oregon. Rob had a relatively undistinguished career in pro ball, but one evening while sitting in the bull pen with former major leaguer Jim Bouton, who was also on the club, the two developed the concept for a new product called "Big League Chew."

Big League Chew, which as you probably know is bubble gum shreds that resemble chewing tobacco and come in a foil packet, got its start in that bull pen in Portland. While Rob Nelson never got to the majors as a pitcher, the annual income from his and Bouton's Big League Chew certainly affords him a major league salary.

Question: Sometimes, in the various baseball publications, I'll see ads announcing new professional leagues or teams. Are those worth checking out?

These new leagues and teams are worth checking out, in more ways than one. Be wary of any new league or team, particularly if as a player you have to pay something up-front. Call or write before committing yourself to anything. You might even want to call or write Major League Baseball in New York City to see if this team or league is legitimate.

This is not to say that such leagues and teams are not worth pursuing. But as with any new venture, make certain you do your homework before signing anything or putting any of your money into their pockets.

Question: Some kids play ball overseas, such as in Italy or Holland. Is that another way of being seen by the scouts?

No, not really. If you opt to play ball in Italy, Holland, Australia, South Africa, or even Mexico or Japan, you're actually limiting your chances of being scouted. While playing ball in another country can be a great deal of fun, if you are trying to make a step into a professional career, you're going in the wrong direction.

If you want to keep pursuing a professional career here in the United States but are no longer eligible to play in the collegiate leagues, hook up with a semipro team that plays an extensive and competitive schedule. Lots of guys 21, 22, and even 23 years old have been signed as undrafted free agents based upon their play in the semipro leagues.

Question: But what about the shortstop with the Los Angeles Dodgers? He's from Australia, and he got signed.

That's Craig Shipley, and yes, he's a native Australian who grew up playing baseball in Parramatta, New South Wales, Australia. He went to Epping High School in Sydney.

But even with a scouting system as extensive as the Dodgers' is, they don't claim to have discovered Shipley down under. The Dodgers didn't become aware of Shipley until he was playing for the University of Alabama. He came to Alabama as a member of a touring Australian team and was offered a baseball scholarship. Shipley, by the way, is the first Australian to play in the big leagues in 85 years.

Question: Why do the scouts at tryout camps rarely give anybody a pat on the back?

It's not that scouts are naturally mean, or always get up on the wrong side of the bed, or don't recognize when a youngster makes an outstanding play or hits a pitch right on the button. But during an audition session, which is what a tryout camp really is, scouts say little to the ballplayers in attendance.

Why is that? Imagine how you would feel if a scout came over to the player next to you and started praising him to the sky, telling him that he was a real prospect, a real potential major leaguer. Naturally, you would expect the scout to say the same kinds of things to you. But suppose he didn't. He complimented your colleague and then looked at you and said nothing, or said things that weren't as complimentary. You'd come away thinking that the scout either didn't know what he was doing or that he was a real louse. Either way, you would be hurt, demotivated, and angry at the scout and his organization. Thus, to avoid hurt feelings and damage to public relations, scouts at tryout camps rarely say anything complimentary.

If the scout is thinking to himself that you're a real find, he'll put your name in his book to follow up. Even though you're accustomed to hearing instant positive feedback from your coach or teammates for a play well made, don't assume the worst if a scout says nothing; in a tryout camp, that doesn't necessarily mean you're not a prospect.

Question: What if my dad or mom talks to the scout after my tryout?

My colleagues tend to be split on the issue of inquiring parents. Some scouts feel that parents have no right to interfere with a scout's analysis of their ball-playing son. Others feel that parents shouldn't get involved until the scout's organization has decided to make an offer to a youngster.

The attitude of these scouts is, Do your parents go and sit on a job interview with you? Do they ask the interviewer whether you got the job? While this attitude may seem harsh, you can understand that it is time-consuming for scouts to answer all the questions that interested parents have about their son's ability.

However, being a parent myself, I can certainly understand the concerns and interest that a father or mother may show for a young man. When a parent approaches me after tryout camp or at a game to ask my professional opinion about his or her son's potential as a prospect, I will typically give it.

I'm not suggesting that you should urge mom and dad to stroll over to the scouts and start asking about your ability. The last thing you want is a notation in the scout's notebook that your parents are "pushy" or "nosy."

But if a parent comes up to me and wants an answer to a specific question or two, I'll be as cordial as my time allows. For example, parents may ask whether I believe their son is good enough to play baseball in a major college program, or whether he'd be better off going to a Division III school or junior college instead. Or they might ask whether I think that their son truly has a chance in the free agent draft or if he should think about attending college in the fall.

These kinds of questions are legitimate ones, and as a scout and father, I feel they deserve honest answers. After all, if I don't tell parents the truth as I see it, they may allow their son to pursue a goal that is either unreachable or, at best, blocked by major obstacles. The answers may not be the ones the parents or the son want to hear. A father may want to hear that his son is going to be a top draft choice and future major leaguer. But if I feel that his son won't be drafted any higher than the 20th round, for example, I feel obligated to tell him so.

Naturally, I'll cushion my answer so as not to embarrass myself or the father. For example, I may say that there are 25 other teams who might feel differently about his son's draftability than I do. But there's really no reason or motivation for me to give a parent anything but my honest assessment. Particularly when the picture is clouded by potential college scholarship offers and the like, the decision is too important to be sidestepped by a scout.

If your parents really want to address a scout about your ability, they should be prepared to ask specific questions. Inquiries such as, "What do you think of my son?" or, "Did you know my boy was selected all-league this year?" are likely to bring a menacing glance from any scout. But if your mom or dad approaches the scout in a more direct, common-sense manner, chances are you'll get a decent response.

Question: How about if I go up to a major league scout myself and ask for an evaluation of my abilities?

Chances are that you'll get the same kind of reaction as was just described. That is, if you are courteous, polite, professional, and specific in your questioning, the scout will probably give you specific answers.

By the same token, if you merely ask the scout for his overall opinion of your abilities, he's liable to be somewhat vague and noncommittal. And he may even tell you things that you didn't ask to hear, such as he's not interested in signing you.

However, as I pointed out earlier, particularly if you're a senior in college, you have little to lose by approaching a scout. If you decide on this kind of direct approach, tell the scout exactly what your status is and how much you really want to play pro ball.

A few years ago a very talented lefty first baseman named Mark Bingham played at Harvard. Bingham, who stands 6'6", had been drafted out of high school by the Cincinnati Reds and supposedly had turned down a bonus of nearly $40,000 to attend Harvard. Although Mark had an outstanding career there, for some reason the New England scouts never drafted him, and by the time he graduated, he was ready to give up his hopes of playing pro ball. But as one last shot, Bingham contacted me and asked me directly if I might be interested in signing him.

I had known about Mark since his high school days and had followed his success in college. As it turned out, the Angels needed a left-handed first sacker for one of their rookie clubs. I made a call to the front office, got their approval, and within 24 hours of his call, Mark was offered a pro contract. That summer he was named to the all-star squad in the Northwest League.

Mark Bingham's story isn't unique. Ray Chadwick, a right-handed pitcher for the Angels, pitched in the majors for the first time in the summer of 1985. Ray had been an outstanding football defensive back at Winston-Salem State in North Carolina. Unfortunately, the school didn't have a baseball team, so he didn't play that sport in college.

However, while Ray was working as part of the grounds crew for the Winston-Salem Red Sox in the Class A Carolina League a few years later, the word got around that he had been a pretty fair pitcher in high school. Angels' scout Alex Cosmides heard the tip, and Ray and Alex talked. After a few workouts, Alex recommended that the Angels draft and sign Ray, which they did. An unusual story, but a true one.

Question: What if I'm invited to an MLSB tryout?

By all means, go, and take the tryout seriously. Remember that your goal is to get on some ballclub's follow-up list. If you do well for the MLSB, your abilities will be reported to the Bureau's headquarters and there is a good chance that the 26 major league club scouting directors will see your name and numbers.

If a scout from the MLSB asks you to fill out a card, by all means, do so. The card will ask for the same basic information that was listed on a typical card from a regular scout (Chapter 2, Figure 2.2). That card will go back to the MLSB front office, be put into a computer, and then be sent out to the major league teams. From there, each team can send its own scout to follow up.

Question: What if I have a "bad day" at an MLSB tryout camp—does that mean that a negative report will be sent to all 26 teams?

MLSB scouts are not so much interested in whether you get a base hit or strike out two batters in a row at a tryout camp. Rather, MLSB scouts, like all scouts, are looking for physical tools—the tools a prospect needs to make it to the majors. Hence, your individual performance, while certainly noticed, is not as important as your skills: running, throwing, bat speed, and pitching control and velocity. Those are the tools MLSB scouts are looking for.

Can an MLSB scout actually sign a player? No, because he's not working for just one club. But on the other hand, some scouts from the Bureau do carry tremendous weight and enjoy great respect from the various ballclubs, and some clubs will gamble on a prospect just because they value that MLSB scout's opinion.

Question: Sometimes a scout tells a ballplayer that he's definitely going to be drafted, but he isn't. How and why does that happen?

Unless you're considered by all the scouts and all the major publications as a definite first-round pick, don't assume that you're going to be drafted. The stands are full of guys who were told directly by a scout that they would definitely be drafted. Then draft day comes, and the telephone never rings.

So while it's nice to hear a scout tell you or your parents that you're a lock to be drafted, it's never a sure thing until you get that actual phone call or telegram from the team's front office, confirming your selection.

Why would a scout be tempted to tell you all this in the first place? That's difficult to say. Perhaps he has so befriended you and your family that in his enthusiasm he has proclaimed, "You're definitely going to be drafted," even when he should know better than to make such promises.

Or maybe, the scout tells you that you're going to be drafted just so he can then ask, "Tell me, how much would it take to sign you?" By making you feel good and then asking your price, he's straying into what most scouts would consider unethical territory.

Sometimes the scout honestly feels that you're going to be drafted and says so. He bases his opinion on the fact that you're the top-rated player on his prospect list. But even that can be misleading, and the scout should know better. As you have read earlier, each scout has a list of top players. But maybe the cross-checker has watched you play and considers you no better than 20th or 25th overall on his master list, even though you're the best prospect in your area.

As a result, by the time the other top prospects have been drafted, your name may fall to the bottom and maybe even off the list, and you don't get drafted. You're embarrassed, and the scout is embarrassed. Again, don't presume anything until the draft comes and you're actually asked to sign.

Question: Is it a good idea not to give your real age?

You may have heard old stories about players who shaved years off their age to convince managers that they were younger than was true. Great players like Satchel Paige, Luis Tiant, Pete Rose are famous for not giving their correct ages.

A ballplayer's age is vitally important to a scout, because all of his calculations and projections about your development are based on what you can do now and your current age. In other words, if you show talents and abilities at age 18 that are more common to a 21-year-old, the scout bases his predictions on that.

By the same token, if you're already 23 and the scout compares your abilities to those of a typical 19-year-old, that affects his evaluation differently. Hence, a player's age is crucial to a scout's judgment, which is why many ballplayers are tempted to subtract a year or two from their real ages.

But you can understand that a scout would be distressed by a youngster who tried to lie about his birthdate or age. As far as scouts are concerned, any time you mislead them or present confusing information about your personal life, you become more of a suspect than a prospect.

Quite simply—don't lie or make any misleading statements to scouts.

Question: Why do so many players get drafted, play for a year, and then get released?

One of the realities of the business side of professional baseball is the limitation of open spots on a roster. The typical major league ballclub has AAA and AA clubs, one or two Class A clubs, and probably a short-season rookie team.

Look at the numbers: In the minors, most clubs are limited to 22–25 active players. That means that from top to bottom, the entire roster of players in one major league system might break down like this:

Major league roster: 24
AAA roster: 23
AA roster: 22–23
Class A rosters (2 teams): 50
Rookie team roster: 30–40
Total: 149–160

The numbers start to get crunched each spring when a new draft is announced. Let's say a typical ballclub drafts 35 new players, of which 30 sign contracts to play. Then perhaps 10 more new players are signed as free agents.

Now the club has 40 new faces, and they want to see them play. A little arithmetic tells you that if 40 new kids are signed, 40 "old" kids have to be released. Since the more talented and proven players are in AAA and AA ball, most clubs release kids from Class A and rookie ball.

The turnover rate is about 20% each spring—quite high for most businesses. But in baseball, it's the only way to stay in the business.

Question: Should a player sign right out of high school or play college ball?

This is a difficult question to answer, because each ballplayer is different from the next. Some kids are definitely better off signing now, while some others are better off to wait. However, the longer a ballplayer waits to play against professional competition, the longer it will take to get to the big leagues.

Here are some of the factors you and your family should take into consideration in making your decision:

How high a draft choice are you? If you're a top draft choice and the club is offering you a substantial signing bonus, then the issue is primarily economic.

Has your physical development peaked? Most ballplayers, at 18 or 19, still have more growing to do. If you don't feel that you've fully matured when offered a contract, perhaps you ought to think about playing college ball for the next few years. Remember, you can always sign after you finish college.

Are you college material academically? If not, you might want to sign now and get a start in pro ball. In other words, if you're not a very good student, attending college just to play ball will not be much motivation in the classroom.

Signing a contract out of high school is often a difficult decision for a young man to make. Make certain you check out all the options before you sign on the dotted line.

Question: What kinds of questions should a high school or junior college player ask of a college coach who comes to recruit?

Assuming that you're satisfied with the school's academic opportunities and campus life—and those are vitally important considerations—the first question I would ask is, "What are my chances of becoming a starter on your club this year?"

You should go on to ask him how many other players he's recruiting at your position, who played your position last season, and how many guys at your position are ahead of you; that is, if you're a freshman second baseman, is the incumbent second baseman a senior or a sophomore?

If the player at your position is only one year ahead, you don't want to sit on the pines waiting for a chance to play only in your senior year.

Ask about the practice schedule, the team's fall and spring game schedules, the off-season weight or conditioning regimen, and any spring trip to the south. Ask any questions you have, and make certain you get answers you can understand. Selecting a college may be one of the most important decisions you make in life, so take your time and get all the information you need.

Question: Is minor league ball as rough as people say it is?

Another difficult question. In general, it's true that playing minor league ball is not very comfortable.

The stories about all-night bus rides, eating in cheap restaurants, and staying in cheap motels are for the most part true. And the pay in the low minors isn't great.

But despite the obstacles, I've found that every young man who ever signed and played pro ball wouldn't have passed up that experience for anything in the world. Remember, you're getting paid to play baseball—and for most ballplayers, that's a dream come true.

Question: What is the role of the scout after he signs a ballplayer?

A scout likes to keep track of his signees. He may talk to a ballplayer weekly by telephone or keep track of his statistics through the club's front office. Scouts take great pride in the players they sign, and certainly enjoy it whenever a young pro takes the time to keep up the communication.

Appendix A

Major League Rules

Rule 3
ELIGIBILITY TO SIGN PLAYER CONTRACT, CONTRACT TERMS, RESERVE LISTS AND CONTRACT RENEWAL TENDERS

(a)   ELIGIBILITY TO SIGN PROFESSIONAL BASEBALL CONTRACTS

Subject to the provisions of the High School, College, Junior College and American Legion Rules listed below, clubs may contract with players under the following circumstances:

1. A player who has not previously contracted with a Major League or National Association club, and who is a resident of the United States, may be signed to a contract only after having been eligible for selection in the Amateur Free Agent Draft as described in Rule 4. A student shall be considered a "resident of the United States" if he academically enrolls in a U.S. high school or college or has a residence located in any of the 50 states, or in the District of Columbia on the date of his contract or within one (1) year prior to said date.

2. A player who has not previously contracted with a Major League or National Association club, who is not a resident of the United States, and who is not subject to the High School, College, Junior College, or American Legion Rules, may be signed to a contract if he:

    (1) Has attained his seventeenth birthday at the time of signing, or

    (2) Is sixteen at the time of signing, but will attain age 17 prior to either the conclusion of the effective season for which he has signed, or September 1 of such effective season, whichever date is later.

    Proof of age in the form of a birth certificate or other appropriate documentation, issued by an appropriate Government Agency, shall accompany the filing of such player's first professional contract with a Major League or National Association club. Major League or National Association clubs who recruit

---

From the *Baseball Blue Book,* P.O. Box 40847, St. Petersburg, FL 33743, pp. 17–22, 39–43, 518–535. Used with permission.

such players may not sign or encourage such players to sign a professional baseball contract other than with a Major League or National Association club.

3. A player who has previously contracted with a Major League or National Association club, and is currently reserved by such club or another assignee club, may be signed to a contract only by the club that currently holds reservation rights to the player's contract.
4. A player who has previously contracted with a Major League or National Association club and who is no longer subject to reservation by a club because he has been granted an unconditional release or becomes a free agent under the terms of a player contract, the Basic Agreement, or these rules, may contract with any club subject to any limitations on re-signing with a prior club.

(b) UNIFORM CONTRACT

To preserve morale and to produce the similarity of conditions necessary to keen competition, the contracts between all clubs and their players in the Major League shall be in a single form. No club shall make a contract different from the uniform contract or a contract containing a non-reserve clause, except with the written approval of the Commissioner. All contracts shall be in duplicate and the player shall retain a counterpart original. The making of any agreement between a club and a player not embodied in the contract shall subject both parties to discipline; and no such agreement, whether written or verbal, shall be recognized or enforced.

No player shall participate in any championship game until he has signed a uniform contract for services during the current season.

No contract shall be approved by the President of the League that shall provide for the giving of a bonus for playing, pitching or batting skill; or which provides for the payment of a bonus contingent on the standing of the club at the end of the championship season.

No club or club official shall make any payment or convey anything of value to any firm or person for legal, representational or other services provided by such firm or person to a player in connection with the negotiation of a contract between such club and player.

No contract of a first-year professional player selected in the summer selection meeting may be assigned outright to a non-affiliated club or organization during the period of one (1) year from the date of the original contract.

(c) HIGH SCHOOL, COLLEGE, JUNIOR COLLEGE AND AMERICAN LEGION RULES

The following rules shall govern contacts, tryouts and eligibility of players subject to selection at the Amateur Free Agent Draft.

CONTACTS

Nothing herein shall be construed as prohibiting any Major League or National Association club, its officers, agents or employees from talking to any player at any time concerning a career in professional baseball and discussing the merits of his contracting, when eligible therefor, with any particular club. However, no discussions shall be held with players during practice sessions or during the progress of games.

Any club, club official, employee, agent or representative thereof, who suggests, procures or otherwise influences a student to withdraw from high school or college, or to refrain from playing college baseball, or to transfer to another college, shall be held in violation of this rule and subject to penalties.

TRYOUTS

During the course of a year, tryouts may be held in accordance with the following:

High School Players

(A) During Summer Vacation. "Tryouts" of high school students may be conducted during the summer vacation period by any Major League or National Association club without permission of any high school official or other restriction.

(B) During School Year. Students may be invited to tryouts during the school year, provided that (1) the Principal of his high school, if not employed by a Major League or National Association club, shall have approved such participation in writing, and (2) any such tryout must be limited to not more than five (5) high school students.

College and Junior College Players

(A) During Summer Vacation. Tryouts of college players by Major League and National Association clubs may be conducted during the summer vacation periods falling between school years, without the permission of any college official or other restriction.

(B) During School Year. No college player shall be tried out by any Major League or National Association club during the school year. However, club officials and scouts shall have the full right to observe players under intercollegiate competition, as they may desire.

(C) Participation in Summer Baseball. In pursuance of the principle that this Rule seeks to protect the eligibility of college players during the college year and at the same time to afford such players every opportunity to develop for possible future professional play, the Major League-National Association College Player Committee is hereby empowered to act on behalf of professional baseball to: (1) survey and investigate the existence of and conditions in summer amateur baseball leagues available to college players; (2) cooperate with the National Collegiate Athletic Association or committees representing that body; and (3) recommend action or legislation to the Commissioner and President of the National Association, all with the objective of extending, liberalizing, and improving the summer amateur baseball program for college age players in the continental United States and Canada.

American Legion Players
Tryouts of American Legion players may be conducted by a club at any time, provided, however, that (a) no such player shall be permitted to participate in any such tryout if such participation would interfere with any of his American Legion activities, and such tryout will be permitted only with a letter of approval from either his Legion coach or the Commander of the Legion post he represents in Legion Play.

PROHIBITION OF EXPENSE PAYMENTS
Nothing whatsoever shall be paid or given any high school or college student, or American Legion player, directly or indirectly, in connection with any tryout, and no club shall reimburse any participant for any travel expenditure in connection with any tryout, nor shall any club enter into any agreement for the future services of any high school or college student at any such tryout.

ELIGIBILITY OF PLAYERS SUBJECT TO RULE

High School Rule in the United States.
No student of a high school in the fifty (50) states of the United States of America or in the District of Columbia shall be signed to a contract by a Major League or National Association club during the period the student is eligible for participation in high school athletics.

EXCEPTION: A player may be signed to a contract which does not obligate him to report for service prior to graduation of the class with which he originally entered high school (until eight (8) semesters after his original entry into the ninth grade), if his eligibility has expired prior to the student's graduation from high school because (a) of student's age, (b) he has completed the maximum number of semesters of attendance, or (c) the maximum number of seasons has passed in which he was eligible to participate in any major sport.

A student who drops out of high school prior to expiration of his athletic eligibility and continues to remain out for at least one (1) year (365 days including the date of withdrawal) may thereafter be signed to a contract for immediate service.

High School Rule in Canada and Puerto Rico
No student of a high school in Canada or Puerto Rico shall be signed to a contract by a Major League or National Association club until (a) he has completed grade eleven of his senior high school curriculum, or (b) he has attained his seventeenth (17) birthday prior thereto, or (c) he has dropped out of school and continued to remain out for at least one year (365 days including the date of withdrawal); provided, however, that if he becomes eligible to sign under either (a) or (b) he may sign a contract which does not obligate him to report for services prior to the termination of the current school year.

College Player Rule
Definition of "College". For the purposes of this Rule the word "college" shall mean any university or other institution of higher education located in the fifty (50) states of the United States of America or District of Columbia, including but not limited to, all members of the National Collegiate Athletic Association and the NAIA, which confers degrees upon students following completion of sufficient credit hours to equal a four-year course, provided the college is represented by a baseball team which participates in intercollegiate competition.

Except as set forth in the EXCEPTIONS to this Rule, no player who is a member (or, if a Freshman, a prospective member) of a baseball team which represents a college in intercollegiate competition may be signed by a Major League or a National Association club during the period beginning with the date he attends the first class in his Freshman year and ending with the graduation of the class with which he originally entered college.

A college student shall be considered to be a member of the baseball team of his college if—

(A) he is a Freshman in a college, whether his college does or does not have an intercollegiate freshman baseball program. Or;

(B) he is a Sophomore (second scholastic year), Junior (third scholastic year), or a Senior (fourth scholastic year), and is a member (or a prospective member) of the varsity baseball squad.

NCAA and NAIA Tournaments. No college player whose team is eligible for the national tournaments conducted by the National Collegiate Athletics Association and the National Association of Intercollegiate Athletics may be signed until the day after his team has been eliminated from such tournament.

EXCEPTIONS. This Rule shall not apply:

(A) To any player who has attained his twenty-first (21) birthday and is currently between school years;

(B) To any player who has completed his Junior year and is currently between school years;

(C) To any player who has completed the full period of eligibility for intercollegiate baseball;

(D) To any player whose association with his college has been terminated by reason of scholastic deficiency;

(E) To any player who withdraws from college and remains out for at least one hundred twenty (120) days (including the date of withdrawal).

Procedure. A college player who is qualified to sign a contract under (A), (B), (C) or (E) above, may, following a Rule 4 Draft, do so without permission of any baseball or college official. A college player who desires to sign a contract by reason of qualifying under the exception set forth in (D) above, or because he is not a member of a team as set forth in this rule, shall make written application to the Commissioner (if he desires to sign a Major League contract) or to the President of National Association (if he desires to sign a National Association contract), setting forth the details of his case and requesting that he be authorized to sign. Should the Commissioner or the President of the National Association decide that an exception is warranted, the player will be notified to that effect.

Junior College Players

No student at a junior college in the United States may be signed during the period commencing with the day he attends the first class of the fall semester of the institution in which he enrolls and ending the day after his team's eligibility during that school year for any regional or national tournament ends.

American Legion Players

1. NO PLAYER ON AN AMERICAN LEGION BASEBALL TEAM shall be signed to a professional baseball contract nor shall any club enter into any agreement for the future services of any American Legion player until the player ceases to be eligible for American Legion competition.
2. (A) In all states and the District of Columbia, clubs may contract with such player until midnight June 30 if the player has attained his seventeenth (17th) birthday prior to January 1 of the current year. After June 30, a club may contract with such player at 12:01 A.M. of the day following his team's final game including tournament play, provided that the player has attained or will have attained his seventeenth (17th) birthday prior to the next January 1.

   (B) No player having started actual competition in the Legion program can be signed after June 30 until eligible as provided in paragraph (A) above.

EXCEPTION: IN ANY CASE WHERE, in the judgment of the Commissioner and the National Americanism Commission of the American Legion having supervision of American Legion Baseball with which a player is or was formerly connected, the facts, circumstances and conditions justify an exception being made to the foregoing and permit the signing of such player to a professional baseball contract, the Commissioner shall so notify all Major League and National Association clubs, and such player may be signed to a professional baseball contract fifteen (15) days subsequent to the date of the Commissioner's notice.

(d) **CONTRACTS IN VIOLATION**

Any contract made in violation of these rules shall be declared null and void, and the official, scout or employee of the offending club who participated in the violation shall be subject to such penalties as the Commissioner or the President of the National Association, as the case may be, may impose.

In addition, if the violation is of the High School, College, or Junior College rule, the offending club (and any club owned by or affiliated with such club) shall be prohibited from signing such player for a period of three (3) years from the date of declaration of voidance of such contract, and shall be fined One Thousand Dollars ($1,000) by the Commissioner if a Major League club or Five Hundred Dollars ($500) by the President of the National Association if a National Association club.

If the violation is of the American Legion Rule, and any club fails to establish that it did not know, and by exercising reasonable care and diligence could not have known, that the player was connected with American Legion Baseball and still eligible therefor, the club shall be fined Five Hundred Dollars ($500) and shall be permanently prohibited from contracting with such player, and, any club official, employee or agent who contracts with such player in violation of the foregoing and who fails to establish that he did not know, and by exercising reasonable care and diligence could not have known of such player's American Legion Baseball service and eligibility, may be declared ineligible by the Commissioner for one (1) year. A written statement by the National Americanism Commission of the American Legion that a player is not connected with American Legion Baseball or has ceased to be eligible therefor, supported by an affidavit by a player or either or both of his parents, that he has not been connected with American Legion Baseball or that, if connected, he has ceased to be eligible for American Legion Baseball by reason of age as shown by date of birth set forth in such affidavit, shall preclude the imposition of any penalty upon the club or club official, employee or agent, but if subsequently ascertained to be incorrect, shall not preclude the Commissioner from declaring the contract null and void.

(e) CONTRACT TERMS FOR FIRST-YEAR PLAYER CONTRACTS

The following terms must be included in each such contract:

(1) First Contract Season. Players who sign following selection at the Summer Meeting must be contracted for either the current or the next succeeding season.

(2) Salary. The salary offered in contracts under this Rule shall be as follows:

(A) Major Leagues—at least Seven Hundred Dollars ($700) per month, the Major League minimum salary rule to apply to actual service in Major Leagues.

(B) All other National Association classifications—seven hundred dollars ($700) per month provided, however, in the event the player is retained on the Active List of a Class AAA or Class AA club for a minimum of thirty (30) days, his salary may be increased up to Eight Hundred Fifty Dollars ($850) per month, at the discretion of the club. Any such salary increases may be retroactive to the first day of active service with Class AAA or Class AA club.

One month's salary shall be guaranteed in all cases.

(3) Trial Period. Each player must receive a trial of fifteen (15) days, during the championship season if the player signs for the current season, or during the spring training period if he signs for the succeeding season. Participation in Instructional League baseball shall not be counted against the fifteen (15) day trial period.

Upon the agreement of both the club and the player, the following terms may be included in each such contract:

(a) Bonus Payments for Signing Contract—Deferred Bonus. All payments due the player or any other person in connection with his signing shall be set forth in the contract and no such payment or installment thereof, shall be deferred beyond conclusion of the calendar year which next follows the date of the contract.

(b) Contingently Postponed Payments Restricted—A player selected under this Rule may be offered a specified sum contingent upon his retention for a stipulated number of days or on a specified date not to exceed ninety (90) days of the club's playing season or seasons provided, however, that such contingently postponed sums shall not exceed Two Thousand Five Hundred Dollars ($2,500.00). Should a contract containing such a provision be selected under Professional Baseball Rule 5 or Article 27, National Association Agreement, prior to the date the bonus becomes payable, the bonus shall become due immediately and shall be paid by the selectee club.

(c) Incentive Bonus Plan—A club may agree to make standard ''Incentive Bonus Payments'' to any player who never before has signed an approved contract with a Major League or National Association club, such payments to be made following retention of the player on the Active List of a club or clubs of certain classifications, or of a higher classification, for ninety (90) days of any one regularly scheduled season, including any official play-off or other post-season series in which the player might be eligible to participate. The amount of such Incentive Bonus Payment and the classification in which they are to be paid are as follows:

If retained by a Class AA Club, the sum of $1,000.00

If retained by a Class AAA club, the sum of $1,500.00

If retained by a Major League club, the sum of $5,000.00

A Major League or Class AAA club shall add to its Incentive Bonus Payment any Incentive Bonus Payment, or payments, the player has not already received from a lower classification club or clubs, regardless of the service, if any, the player has had in such lower classification or classifications.

Time spent on any Inactive List shall not be counted toward the ninety (90) days required to be served before an Incentive Bonus Payment becomes payable; provided, however, that if a player is placed on the Disabled List after he has been credited with sixty (60) or more days of service in any particular season, the Disabled List time shall be counted to his credit. Time spent on optional or conditional assignment shall not be counted toward such ninety (90) days unless the assignment be to a classification qualified for Incentive Bonus Payment, in which event such time shall be counted toward the payment applicable to the classification of the assignee club. .

A player who has received the Incentive Bonus Payment applicable to a particular classification shall not thereafter be entitled to another such payment for service in the same classification, whether such service occurs in the same or a subsequent season.

Liability for Payments. The club which holds a player's contract at the time an Incentive Bonus Payment becomes due shall pay such bonus to the player.

Unconditional release of the player or free agency shall terminate the Incentive Bonus Plan insofar as he is concerned.

(d) College Scholarship Plan—A club may agree through the College Scholarship Plan, to pay on behalf of a player who never before has signed an approved contract with a Major League or National Association club, the costs incident to his attendance at an accredited college of his choice for tuition, room, board, books and fees, subject to the following:

1. Not more than Twelve Thousand Dollars ($12,000.00) shall be paid on behalf of any one player and not more than Fifteen Hundred Dollars ($1,500.00) thereof shall be paid in any one (1) semester.
2. The player must be enrolled in a fulltime course (minimum of 10 credit hours if on a quarter system; 12 credit hours if on a semester system) at an accredited college or university and must have com-

menced his studies in such course within eighteen (18) months after date of his signing of the contract.

When Club Relieved of Payments. Unconditional release of the player or his placement on the Military List shall not relieve the club of the obligation to make such payments but the club shall be relieved of such obligation should the player:

1. Fail to attend college for two (2) consecutive years without proper reason, in the judgment of the Commissioner; or
2. Be placed on the Ineligible List.

Major League Players. A Major League player for whom there is in effect on or after January 1, 1973 a valid and unexpired scholarship under the College Scholarship Plan may commence or resume his studies under the Plan at any time within two (2) years after his last day of Major League service. If his college studies have not commenced under the Plan by that date, his scholarship shall terminate. If he has commenced his studies by that date his scholarship shall continue unless he shall fail to attend college for more than two (2) consecutive years after that date, without proper reason. Participation by a Player in Winter League or Instructional League play shall constitute proper reason for tolling the time limitation in the preceding sentence.

Liability for Payments. If the club which originally signs the player is affiliated with a Major League club at the time the player is signed and the Major League club approved the player's participation in the Plan, such Major League club shall be liable to make the payments incident to the Plan whether or not the player's contract is subsequently selected by or assigned (outright, optionally or conditionally) to a club outside the organization of such Major League club; provided, however, that in case of assignment otherwise than by selection, or on waiver claim, the assignee club may agree, through a statement set forth in the assignment agreement, to undertake to make any payments which accrue subsequent to date of such assignment. If the original club is not affiliated with a Major League club, it shall continue to be liable to make the Plan payments should the player's contract be selected or assigned; provided, however, that, in case of assignment otherwise than by selection or on waiver claim, the assignee club may agree, through a statement set forth in the assignment agreement, to undertake to make any payments which accrue subsequent to date of such assignment.

Administration. The Plan shall be supervised by the Commissioner, or by an Administrator appointed by him, and all payments made under the Plan shall be made by the Commissioner, or by such Administrator, but the club liable for the payments in accordance with the above paragraph shall reimburse the Commissioner's office promptly upon receipt of billing to cover such payments. All payments under the Plan shall be made to the college attended by the player.

Procedure. A Club which agrees to participation of a player in the Plan shall enter a statement in the contract such as "Player is to participate in the College Scholarship Plan established by Professional Baseball Rule 3, receipt of copy of which Plan is hereby acknowledged by the player." Copy of the Plan shall be delivered to the player at the time his signature is taken to the contract and, upon receipt of notification that the contract has been approved, the Commissioner shall inform the player that his inclusion in the Plan has been approved and furnish him with an additional copy of it, together with instructions as to the procedure to be followed.

(4) The following provisions may not be included in such contracts:

(a) Multi-Season Contracts. No contract signed under this Rule, whether for a player's first year of service, or any subsequent National Association contract, may be for a term of more than one (1) season (exclusive of renewal options).

(b) "Percentage" and "Stipulated Sum" Payments. No contract, or any renewal thereof, with a player selected under Rule 4 shall include a provision for payment of a "percentage" of the consideration or of a "stipulated sum" upon assignment of the contract.

TERMS ACCEPTED. Any agreement between club and player for service, evidenced by written acceptance, whether by letter or telegram, or receipt from player for money advanced to him to bind such agreement, shall be construed to be a contract and held to be binding, provided the player declines to enter into a formal contract. The player's refusal to sign such formal contract shall disqualify him from playing with the contracting club or entering the service of any Major League or National Association club unless released or assigned.

FILING OF CONTRACTS AND TERMS ACCEPTED. The validity of any contract, arrangement, or agreement between a club and a player not on its Reserve List for the service of the player will not be recognized unless the written proof thereof is submitted (to the President of the interested club's league, and to the Commissioner) within twenty (20) days after such agreement is made, for promulgation in the next official bulletin, and unless the agreement is actually approved.

(f) FILING OF RESERVE LISTS

On or before November 20 in each year, each Major League club shall transmit to the Commissioner and to its League President a list not exceeding forty (40) active and eligible players, whom the club desires to reserve for the ensuing season; and also a list of all its players who have been promulgated as placed on the Military, Voluntarily Retired, Restricted, Disqualified, Suspended or Ineligible Lists; and players signed under Rule 4 who do not count in the club's under control limit. On or before November 30 the League President shall transmit all of said lists to the Secretary-Treasurer of the Executive Council, who shall thereupon promulgate same, and thereafter no player on any list shall be eligible to play for or negotiate with any other club until his contract has been assigned or he has been released.

EXCEPTION. In any year when the World Series is scheduled to end on or after October 12, or where inclement weather delays the playing of the final game to or beyond October 12, the Commissioner may designate later final dates than those set forth in this Rule 3 for the filing of Reserve Lists.

Selector clubs, under a Player Development Contract, may transmit to the President of the National Association and to the President of the selectee club's league, a Reserve List of the selectee club to be accepted with regard to players subject to the selector club's right of selection under a Player Development Contract in the event that the selectee club fails to transmit its Reserve List by the date provided or omits the name or names of any players subject to the selector club's right of selection under a Player Development Contract.

SALARY UNPAID. A club shall have no right to reserve a player to whom it is indebted for arrears in salary as to which no bona fide undecided dispute exists; and upon application by any such player, the Commissioner may remove such player's name from the Reserve List and declare him a free agent.

RETIRED, RESTRICTED, DISQUALIFIED OR INELIGIBLE PLAYERS. A player reserved for two (2) consecutive years on the Voluntarily Retired, Restricted, Disqualified or Ineligible Lists shall be omitted from future Reserve Lists but shall not be eligible until first reinstated in accordance with Major League Rule 16, and upon such reinstatement, he shall be restored to the Active List of the Club with which connected when he retired or became ineligible.

(g) CONTRACT RENEWAL TENDERS

Contracts must be tendered to eligible Major League players on or before December 20 (or if Sunday, then on the preceding business day) and to eligible National Association players on or before March 1 (or if Sunday, then on the succeeding business day), except that tender shall be made by National Association clubs on or before January 15 (or if Sunday, then on the preceding business day) to any player whose contract was acquired by recent assignment from a Major League club, unless the player shall have signed a National Association contract subsequent to such assignment. Such tender may be made to the player in person or by mail addressed to his last address of record with the club. Clubs must tender a contract to any player whose name appears on their reserve lists who is on the Restricted List as a result of either failing to report to his club or failing to contract with it, or who is on the Disqualified List for failure to render his services to his club. Clubs shall not tender a contract to any player whose name appears on their reserve lists who is on the Suspended, Ineligible, Voluntarily Retired or Military List, or who is on the Restricted or Disqualified List for reasons other than those specified in the preceding sentence.

(h) UNIFORM MANAGERS' and EMPLOYEES' CONTRACTS

which contain no reserve clause shall terminate at midnight, November 15, of the "year" set forth in the contract, unless otherwise stipulated therein.

(i) GIFT FOR SECURING EMPLOYMENT FORBIDDEN

If any scout, player, employee or official of any club, or any umpire, employee or official of any league, shall demand or receive any money or other valuable consideration, whether gratuitous or otherwise, from any player or umpire for or because of services rendered, or to be rendered, or supposed to have been rendered, in securing him employment with any Major League or National Association club, such money or other valuable consideration shall be returned immediately upon its receipt, and if not so returned the Commissioner may impose such penalties, including ineligibility, as he may deem proper.

(j) TAMPERING

To preserve discipline and competition, and to prevent the enticement of players, coaches, managers and umpires, there shall be no negotiations or dealings respecting employment, either present or prospective, between any player, coach or manager and any club other than the club with which he is under contract or acceptance of terms, or by which he is reserved or which has the player on its Negotiation List, or between any umpire and any league other than the league with which he is under contract or acceptance of terms, unless the club or league with which he is connected shall have, in writing, expressly authorized such negotiations or dealing prior to the commencement. Managers, coaches, trainers and salaried scouts are required to sign contracts on forms prescribed by the Executive Council before rendering service to a club. (So-called "Bird Dog" scouts and scouts whose compensation is conditional upon performance of players are not required to sign one of the aforementioned contracts. However, such "Bird Dog" and sub-scouts are required to be signed to such contract or agreement as the club may draft.)

Rule 4

AMATEUR FREE AGENT DRAFT

(a) PLAYERS SUBJECT

Clubs may contract with players who are residents of the United States, and who have not previously contracted with a Major League or National Association club, only in accordance with this Rule and the provisions of the High School, College, Junior College or American Legion Rules, if applicable.

(b) SELECTION MEETING

One selection meeting shall be conducted each year on or about June 10, to be known as the "Summer Meeting." The date and place of each meeting shall be fixed by the Commissioner.

(1) Regular and Secondary Phases. Each Meeting shall be conducted in two (2) phases. The First, to be known as the "Regular Phase", shall consist of selection of eligible players who were not selected at the preceding meeting. When clubs of all classifications have completed selections under the Regular Phase, the second phase, to be known as the "Secondary Phase", shall be conducted. The Secondary Phase shall consist of selections of eligible players who are on record in the Commissioner's office as subject to selection because they were not contracted following selection at a previous meeting.

(2) Procedure. The Commissioner shall preside at selections by Major League and Class AAA clubs; the President of the National Association at selections by all other clubs.

Each club shall designate a representative to act in its behalf and such representative may, as the club's turn is called, select a player for the club's Negotiation List.

SELECTION LIMITS. Each club other than Rookie League clubs shall be entitled to select, at each of the Regular and Secondary Phases of each meeting, the following number of players with the exception that all selections in the Secondary Phase shall be confined to Class A clubs only:

Regular Phase

Major League Club	1
Class AAA Club	1
Class AA Club	1
Class A Club—No Limit	

Secondary Phase

Class A Club—No Limit

A club's right to select shall terminate when (1) it has selected its limit or players as set forth above, (2) it has announced a "pass" or (3) it has failed to respond to a call.

The selecting club shall be responsible for determining the eligibility of selected players.

No club may transfer to another club its right to select.

For a period of two years immediately following the date of entry into a Major League by a new club, such club may select in the round of each classification regardless of whether such club has a Player Development Contract in effect for that classification.

(c) PRIORITY OF CLASSIFICATION AND LEAGUES WITHIN CLASSIFICATIONS

Selections by classification shall be made in the following order: Major League, Class AAA, Class AA, Class A.

Major Leagues. The American League shall have priority in all Summer Meetings conducted under this Rule in odd-numbered years and the National League shall have priority in the even-numbered years. In the event one Major League has more clubs than the other Major League, the additional clubs in the League having more clubs shall draft at the end of each round.

A Major League club which has failed to sign its first round selection in the Regular Phase of the preceding Summer Meeting shall have the right to select a player after the completion of the first round, and any first round compensation selections as provided for in the Basic Agreement. Should there be more than one club in this category, the selections will be made in the same order as the Regular Phase.

Class AAA and AA. Class AAA and AA clubs shall make selections in the same order as their Major League affiliates in the same selection meeting. Class AAA and AA clubs without Major League affiliations shall have priority in the order of each selection over Class AAA and AA clubs with Major League affiliations.

Class A. The selection rights of each Class A club shall be exercised by the Major League club with which it is affiliated, and in the same order as the Major League club selects players in selections by Major League clubs. Each Major League club when called in proper order shall name the player who is being selected and the affiliated Class A club for which the selection is being made. There shall be no limit upon the number of selections that may be made on behalf of any one Class A club. In the Regular Phase, Class A clubs without Major League affiliations shall have priority in the order of each selection over Class A clubs with Major League affiliations; in the Secondary Phase such Class A clubs shall have no right to select in the first three rounds but shall have priority in the fourth and succeeding rounds.

(d) CLUB PRIORITIES

(1) Regular Phase. At the Regular Phase Major League clubs shall select in reverse order of their league standing at the close of the preceding season. If the Major Leagues operate on a divisional basis, each club's standing within its league shall be determined by the percentage of games it won, exclusive of any post-season games to determine the divisional or league championship. National Association clubs shall select in accordance with the third and fourth paragraphs of section (c) of this Rule.

(2) Secondary Phase. Selections in the Secondary Phase shall alternate between the Major Leagues in accordance with section (c) and in the groups indicated below, each Major League to determine the selection order of its clubs by lot. National Association clubs shall select in accordance with section (c) of this Rule.

Group A. The following group of clubs shall occupy selection position 1 through 13 at the Summer Meeting in all even-numbered years but shall be in the group occupying position 14 through 26 at the Summer Meeting in all odd-numbered years: Atlanta, California, Cincinnati, Cleveland,

Detroit, Houston, Kansas City, Los Angeles, Milwaukee, New York Mets, San Diego, Seattle and Texas.

Group B. The following group of clubs shall occupy selection position 14 through 26 at the Summer Meeting in all even-numbered years but shall be in the group occupying positions 1 through 13 at the Summer Meeting in all odd-numbered years: Baltimore, Boston, Chicago Cubs, Chicago White Sox, Minnesota, Montreal, New York Yankees, Philadelphia, Oakland, Pittsburgh, St. Louis, San Francisco and Toronto.

A player selected in a Secondary Phase shall have the same status for all purposes as one selected in the Regular Phase.

A player who was eligible for the Secondary Phase but is not selected shall be free to contract with any club at any time prior to the next following Closed Period. If he does not contract in that time, he shall be subject at the Regular Phase of the meeting following the next Closed Period.

Subject to the foregoing, the Commissioner and the President of the National Association shall decide any procedural questions falling within their respective jurisdictions.

(e) EFFECT OF SELECTION ON PLAYER

A selected player shall be placed on the club's Negotiation List and shall remain thereon until start of the Closed Period of the next selection meeting, unless at an earlier date he

Signs a contract;

Is removed because he was not eligible for selection;

Becomes a College Player by entering or returning to college;

Or if the club's Negotiation Right has been revoked under section (f) of this Rule.

Players who join the Armed Forces while on the Negotiation List shall continue to be subject to this Rule in the same manner as all other selected players.

A club shall have exclusive right to contract with a player on its Negotiation List and negotiations must be conducted by the selecting club or by an affiliated club of high classification, provided, however, that the player may, if he so desires, contract with an affiliated club of lower classification.

A club may not transfer its Negotiation Right to any other club.

Players on the Negotiation List shall not count against any player limits.

Negotiations with the player must be conducted in accordance with Rule 3.

(f) NEGOTIATION RIGHTS

Each Major League and National Association club (except clubs of leagues all of whose members are located outside the United States) which selects the rights to negotiate exclusively with players, must, not later than fifteen (15) days after the close of the draft meeting, commence negotiations in any manner the club elects, including correspondence, personal contact or the tender of a formal contract. Upon request of the Commissioner if the club holding the Negotiation Right is a Major League club, or the President of the National Association if the club holding the Negotiation Right is a National Association club, the club must produce documentary evidence of compliance with this provision. Failure to produce such evidence shall void the Negotiation Right and the player shall be free to sign with any club fifteen (15) days after notice has been given all clubs of voidance of the Negotiation Right.

Players who are eligible to contract on the date of the selection meeting, or within forty-five (45) days thereafter, may be selected.

EXCEPTION: American Legion players who will first become eligible to sign, under the American Legion Rule, at the end of their current Legion season, may be selected at the Summer Meeting. Contact with any such player must be made within fifteen (15) days after date of selection, but a contract may not be signed until his Legion team has completed its activities for the year.

(g) CLOSED PERIOD

The seven (7) days preceding the Summer Meeting shall be known as the Closed Period. The right to contract with a player, whether or not selected at the preceding meeting, shall terminate at 12:01 a.m. on the seventh (7) day prior to the date of the next Selection Meeting.

EXCEPTION: A college player or junior college player selected at the preceding Summer Meeting, whose team's intercollegiate schedule (including any regional or national tournament) extends past the start of the Closed Period, may be signed during the Closed Period during the interim starting the day after his team's last intercollegiate game and ending at 12:01 a.m. of the day on which the Summer Meeting is scheduled to start. Written or telegraphic evidence of such a signing must be presented prior to commencement of the Secondary Phase of the Summer Meeting.

(h) EFFECT ON PLAYER LIMITS

Summer Meeting. A player who signs for the current season with a club of any classification (including a Major League club) following his selection at the Summer Meeting shall be excluded from the signing club's limit of players under control until date of filing of the Reserve List, but if retained by the contracting club, shall count against that club's active player limit when fifteen (15) days have elapsed from date of the contract or when he has appeared in a Championship game, whichever first occurs. If assigned optionally in such current season by the contracting club, the player shall count immediately against the optionee club's limit of active players but shall not count against the optionor club's limit of optional players. If assigned outright or conditionally, the player shall count immediately against all player limits of the assignee club.

A player selected at the Summer Meeting who signs for the succeeding season shall count against the under control limit of the signing club when fifteen (15) days have elapsed from date of contract, unless the player signs after July 1 with a Class A or Rookie Classification club, in which case he may be carried as one of the 12 "extra" players allowed clubs of those classifications under Professional Baseball Rule 2(b).

(i) IF PLAYER DOES NOT SIGN

A player who does not sign following selection at the Summer Meeting shall become eligible for selection at the Secondary Phase of the next Summer meeting.

If any selected player does not contract prior to the start of the Closed Period next following the meeting at which he was selected, the club shall notify the Commissioner of the fact on the first day of the Closed Period. The player shall be subject to further selection as follows:

1. If the player is next eligible for selection at a meeting held within thirteen (13) months after the date on which he last was selected, he shall be subject to selection in the Secondary Phase.
   EXCEPTION: A college player who is selected at the Summer Meeting solely because of age or completion of his Junior year and returns to college in the Fall without signing, shall be subject to selection in the Regular Phase of the next Summer Meeting.
2. If the player is next eligible for selection at a meeting held more than thirteen (13) months after the date at which he last was selected, he shall be subject to selection in the Regular Phase.
   EXCEPTION: A college player who becomes eligible for selection solely because he has withdrawn from college shall be subject to selection in the Secondary Phase.

A list of all players who have not signed following selection shall be sent to all clubs by the Commissioner as far as possible in advance of each selection meeting. The list shall indicate which players will be subject to selection at the meeting, and in which phase.

A selected player who does not sign may not be selected by the same club or any affiliate thereof in the Regular Phase or Secondary Phase at any subsequent meeting unless he has notified the Commissioner in writing that he has no objection to such re-selection.

(j) IF PLAYER IS NOT SELECTED

A player who is eligible for selection in either phase of any selection meeting and who is not selected may be signed by any club after the selection meeting adjourns until the start of the next following Closed Period.

EXCEPTION: A college player who is eligible for selection solely because of age or completion of his junior year and who is not selected at a Summer Meeting may be signed only during the summer recess between school years. Any such player who returns to college in the Fall without signing shall be subject to selection at the Regular Phase of the next Summer Meeting.

(k) OTHER NEW PLAYERS

The provisions of MLR 3 (e), (3) and (4) shall apply to the contracts of: (1) players who are not subject to selection under Rule 4 (a) (1), (2) players who were subject to selection under Rule 4 (a) (1) at the selection meeting preceding the date of signing but were not selected and (3) players the Negotiation Rights with whom were revoked under the first paragraph of Rule 4 (b). The salary in such contracts with National Association clubs shall not exceed Seven Hundred Dollars ($700.00) per month.

(l) INTERPRETATION

Official interpretations of this Rule may be made from time to time by a committee consisting of the Commissioner, the President of the American League, the President of the National League and the President of the National Association, plus two (2) non-voting club officials, one of whom is to be appointed by the President of the American League and the other by the President of the National League. Should an even division exist between the committee members on any matter before it, the vote of the Commissioner shall determine the committee's action.

SPECIAL AMENDMENT PROVISION. The amendments to Rules 3 and 4 adopted at the annual meetings of November–December 1966 may be repealed by vote of a simple majority of the National Association Leagues instead of the usual three-fourths (3/4) majority, provided the Major Leagues also vote for repeal in accordance with Sec. 2, Art. V., Major League Agreement. Should such amendments be repealed Rules 3 and 4 shall be adjusted to conform with the repeal action.

Appendix B

Addresses

American and National Leagues
350 Park Avenue
New York, NY 10022
(212) 371-7600 (American League)
(212) 371-7300 (National League)

American League

Baltimore Orioles
Memorial Stadium
Baltimore, MD 21218
(301) 243-9800
Executive Vice President and General Manager: Henry J. Peters
Scouting Director: Thomas Giordano

Boston Red Sox
Fenway Park
24 Yawkey Way
(617) 267-9440
Vice President, General Manager: Lou Gorman
Scouting Director: Edward M. Kasko

California Angels
2000 S. State College Blvd.
P.O. Box 2000
Anaheim, CA 92803
(714) 937-6700
Senior Vice President and General Manager: Mike Port
Director, Scouting and Player Development: Bob Fontaine, Jr.

Chicago White Sox
324 W. 35th St.
Chicago, IL 60616
(312) 924-1000
General Manager: Larry Himes
Director of Scouting: Al Goldis

Cleveland Indians
The Stadium, Gate A
Boudreau Blvd.
Cleveland, OH 44114
(216) 861-1200
General Manager: Joe Klein
Director, Player Development and Scouting: Jeff Scott

Detroit Tigers
2121 Trumbull Ave.
Detroit, MI 48216
(313) 962-4000
Vice President and General Manager: William R. Lajoie
Director of Player Development: Joe McDonald

Kansas City Royals
P.O. Box 1969
Kansas City, MO 64141
(816) 921-2200
Executive Vice President and General Manager: John Schuerholz
Director of Scouting and Player Development: Art Stewart

Milwaukee Brewers
201 S. 46th St.
Milwaukee, WI 53214
(414) 933-4114
Executive Vice President and General Manager: Harry I. Dalton
Scouting Director: Dan Duquette

Minnesota Twins
501 Chicago Ave., S.
Minneapolis, MN 55415
(612) 375-1366
General Manager: Andy MacPhail
Director of Scouting: Terry Ryan

New York Yankees
Yankee Stadium
Bronx, NY 10451
(212) 293-4300

Vice President and General Manager: Clyde E. King
Director of Scouting: Brian Sabean

Oakland As
Oakland-Alameda County Coliseum
P.O. Box 2220
Oakland, CA 94621
(415) 638-4900

General Manager: Sandy Alderson
Director of Scouting: Dick Bogard

Seattle Mariners
100 S. King St., Suite 300
P.O. Box 4100
Seattle, WA 98104
(206) 628-3555

General Manager: Dick Balderson
Director of Scouting: Roger Jongewaard

Texas Rangers
1200 Copeland Rd.
P.O. Box 1111
Arlington, TX 76010
(817) 273-5222

Vice President and General Manager: Thomas A. Grieve
Director, Player Development: Sandy Johnson

Toronto Blue Jays
Exhibition Stadium
Exhibition Place
Box 7777
Adelaide St. P.O.
Toronto, Ontario M5C 2K7
(416) 595-0077

General Manager: Pat Gillick
Director of Scouting: Gord Ash

National League

Atlanta Braves
521 Capitol Ave.
Atlanta, GA 30312
(404) 522-7630

General Manager: Robert J. Cox
Vice President, Director of Scouting: Paul Snyder

Chicago Cubs
1060 W. Addison St.
Chicago, IL 60613
(312) 281-5050

President and General Manager: Dallas Green
Director of Scouting: Scott Reid

Cincinnati Reds
100 Riverfront Stadium
Cincinnati, OH 45202
(513) 421-4510

Executive Vice President, General Manager: Bill Bergesch
Director, Scouting: Larry Doughty

Houston Astros
8701 Kirby Dr.
Houston, TX 77054
(713) 799-9500

President and General Manager: Dick Wagner
Director of Scouting: Dan O'Brien, Jr.

Los Angeles Dodgers
1000 Elysian Park Ave.
Los Angeles, CA 90012
(213) 224-1500

General Manager: Fred Claire
Director, Scouting: Ben Wade

Montreal Expos
P.O. Box 500
Station M
Montreal, Quebec H1V 3P2
(514) 253-3434

Vice President and General Manager: Murray Cook
Director of Scouting: Gary Hughes

New York Mets
126th & Roosevelt Ave., Flushing
New York, NY 11368
(718) 507-6387

Executive Vice President and General Manager: J. Frank Cashen
Director of Scouting: Roland Johnson

Philadelphia Phillies
Veterans Stadium
Broad St. & Pattison Ave.
P.O. Box 7575
Philadelphia, PA 19101
(215) 463-6000

General Manager: Bill Giles
Director, Scouting: Jim Baumer

Pittsburgh Pirates
Three Rivers Stadium
600 Stadium Circle
P.O. Box 7000
Pittsburgh, PA 15212
(412) 323-5000

Executive Vice President and General Manager: Sydnor W. Thrift, Jr.
Director of Scouting: Elmer Gray

St. Louis Cardinals
250 Stadium Plaza
St. Louis, MO 63102
(314) 421-3060

General Manager: Dal Maxvill
Director of Scouting: Fred McAlister

San Diego Padres
9449 Friars Rd.
San Diego, CA 92108
(619) 283-7294

General Manager: Jack McKeon
Scouting Director: Tom Romenesko

San Francisco Giants
Candlestick Park
San Francisco, CA 94124
(415) 468-3700

President and General Manager: Al Rosen
Director of Player Personnel and Scouting: Bob Fontaine

Glossary of Common Scouting Terms

Arm speed: Referred to in connection with a pitcher's velocity. That is, if a pitcher is to have good speed on a pitch, he must whip his arm with above-average arm speed. Weak or slow speed invariably means that the pitcher doesn't throw very hard.

Breaking pitch: Anything from a curve to a slider to a split-finger fastball.

Crow hop: A little skip-step that an infielder makes when he has fielded a ball cleanly and has time to make a strong throw to first. The "crow hop" gives the infielder a chance to set his feet straight before throwing.

Free agent draft: Held the first week of June for eligible players, this is major league baseball's system for replenishing its talent pool in the minor leagues. Eligibility rules are a bit tricky and do change occasionally; if you aren't sure whether you're eligible, review the Appendix or check with a local scout in your area.

Gamer: Some ballplayers actually look more like prospects in a real game than in a tryout or pregame workout. These kids are sometimes referred to by scouts as "gamers," or players who tend to bring out their potential during the heat of competition.

Going (went) away: A local ballplayer who has signed and gotten the chance to "go away" to play pro ball.

Good athletic body: Description of a ballplayer who has excellent physique and is well coordinated. Scouts feel more assured signing ball-players who are obviously good athletes as well as good baseball players.

Good baseball instincts: Instincts usually develop only after a youngster has played lots of sandlot, high school, college and other amateur ball. Scouts look for a ballplayer's "instincts" in running the bases, choosing which base to throw to during a play, and anticipating what might happen next in a game. A player with good instincts makes good decisions as he plays.

Good jump on the pitcher: Base stealers study a pitcher's move to the plate in order to anticipate the pitch and get a good jump.

Good mechanics: Usually refers to a pitcher's wind-up and form. Scouts like to see quick, easy, fluid motion. The fewer the moving parts, the less chance of that youngster ever developing an arm problem.

Incentive clause: Some ballclubs put such a clause in a player's initial contract stipulating that he will be rewarded with a specific bonus if he makes it to AA, AAA, or the major leagues. The amount can vary from a few hundred dollars to a few thousand, or more.

Instructional league: At the end of each minor league season (usually around Labor Day), each major league office sends its top prospects to the instructional league to work out under tutelage. This special "season" runs from mid-September to early November. Being invited to the instructional league is considered a great honor by most minor leaguers, as it means that they are seen as bona fide major league prospects.

Just a thrower: A pitcher who throws hard, but with little finesse or accuracy. Throwers usually have enough velocity to get by, but need to learn the finer points of pitching as they mature.

Makes things happen: A ballplayer who makes things happen is a welcome sight to a scout—he's the kid who starts a rally with an unexpected bunt, takes the extra base when nobody expects him to, makes the hustling play in the field. An intangible quality, and a real plus.

Minor league salary: Typically around $700 a month for a five-month season in Class A ball, plus a modest meal allowance for road games. Minor leaguers are not paid for their spring training season.

Movement: A pitch with good movement means the ball is tailing in, tailing out, moving up, or moving down.

Needs a third pitch: Most amateur pitchers have two pitches: the fastball and the curve. That is usually sufficient for amateur ball, but in the professional ranks, good hitters quickly learn to look for either pitch. Scouts will say that a youngster needs a third pitch, such as a slider or change-up, so he'll have more luck keeping professional batters off balance.

O.B. (organized baseball): An older term referring to professional baseball or the minor leagues.

Organization player: Sometimes a scout signs a marginal prospect because the organization happens to need an extra player in that position that season. This player, nonetheless a professional, is called an organization player because he has been selected to fill a role or slot rather than as a major league prospect.

Out pitch: Not necessarily a strikeout pitch, but one thrown to pull the batter off-stride, in hopes of his hitting a ground ball, pop-up, or fly out. The strikeout, of course, is just an added bonus. All professional pitchers have an out pitch that they save to use on a hitter at just the right time.

Patient hitter: A hitter who rarely swings at the first pitch, but waits the pitcher out, allowing several pitches before swinging.

Quick bat: A hitter with a quick bat can wait on a pitch until the very last second and then unleash a stroke powerfully. Ballplayers with quick bats are usually good hitting prospects.

Quick feet: Infielders with quick feet are able to adapt to bad hops or throws and other unexpected events during the course of a play and still keep their balance. One doesn't have to be fast to have quick feet: The term refers more to anticipation and balance than speed. It's another desirable trait scouts look for.

Quick hands: A term usually applied to an infielder or catcher, meaning an ability to adjust rapidly with one's hands to an unexpected bad hop or close play. A shortstop or second baseman with quick hands has the ability to take a tough-to-handle grounder and transform it into a routine out.

Quick release: A catcher with a quick release doesn't take much time receiving the pitch and firing the ball to second base on an attempted steal. A youngster can make up for a fair arm if he's accurate and has a quick release to second. Outfields can be termed as having a quick release after catching fly outs.

Range: Refers to a defensive player's ability to cover a lot of ground. However, one's range means coverage in four different directions—to the left, to the right, frontwards, and backwards. Having excellent range is a key trait that scouts look for in a prospect.

Signing bonus: Different from an incentive clause, a signing bonus is a cash payment made to a prospect, drafted or undrafted, just for signing his name to the professional contract. The bonus normally is given without any requirements on performance.

Singles hitter: Pete Rose is not only the greatest hitter of all time, he was also the greatest singles hitter. Scouts don't use the term negatively as is sometimes thought. Rather, a solid singles hitter is often regarded as a top prospect.

Sleeper: A potential pro player who was uncovered late in his career or passed over by most clubs and then "blossomed" when given a chance. Many sleepers are found at small schools or on the sandlots.

Slow bat: Hitters who tend to get jammed on pitches or loft the ball to the opposite field are sometimes labeled as having a slow bat. The usual feeling among scouts is that if a hitter can't get around on amateur pitching, he'll have even greater problems against major league pitchers.

Slow to the plate: Scouts carefully watch how fast a pitcher delivers to the plate with men on base. A hurler with a big leg kick is invariably slow to the plate, which allows base runners to get big jumps for stealing.

Soft hands: Used primarily to describe infielders and catchers; refers to the ability to receive the ball with little effort and a sense of smoothness and grace. A player with soft hands has "give" in his catching motion as opposed to one with "iron" hands.

Some pop in his bat: A player with this usually has demonstrated, on occasion, the ability to hit the ball with power and for distance.

Suspect: A ballplayer who has all the tools he needs to be a professional player is called a prospect. A ballplayer whose professional potential is questionable is labeled by scouts as a "suspect."

Tablesetter: Usually the first two men in the lineup, whose main job is to get on base—to be the tablesetters for the big RBI hitters batting behind them.

Tuition bonus: Under current rules, a college ballplayer who signs a professional contract and gives up any remaining years of a collegiate scholarship is allowed only $1500 a semester ($3000 a year) from the major league club as a tuition bonus. In other words, if you're a junior at a college that costs $10,000 a year in tuition and other costs, and you are drafted, the professional team can offer you only a maximum of $3000 for your senior year. Of course, other bonus money (signing, incentive, etc.) can be used to pay for your schooling.

Uppercutter: Some youngsters like to think of themselves as home run hitters and have adopted swings in which they "uppercut" like Dave Winfield and Darryl Strawberry. However, scouts realize that people like Winfield and Strawberry are 6'6'', very strong, and very rare; the typical professional hitter doesn't uppercut, but actually swings down on the pitch to hit line drives and hard grounders.

U.R. (unconditional release): Given to a professional player when the front office has decided his services are no longer required. He is free to negotiate as a free agent with any other club interested in him.

Velocity: The raw speed of a pitch, which can be accurately clocked by a radar gun. Velocity does not refer to control, movement, or effectiveness.

Winter ball: Different from the instructional league. Some ballplayers, in hopes of making money from baseball all year round, head south to the Caribbean professional leagues during the winter months to stay in shape and make extra cash. Usually only ballplayers of major league or AAA caliber can find winter-ball employment.

Index

About the Authors

Al Goldis   **Rick Wolff**

AL GOLDIS is the Director of Scouting and Player Development for the Chicago White Sox. A three-sport star at John Bartram High School in Philadelphia, Goldis was signed by the Cincinnati Reds and was considered a top outfield prospect in the Reds' chain before his career was ended prematurely by a torn rotator cuff.

Goldis, who has served as a collegiate coach as well as scout for the Orioles and Angels, graduated from the Philadelphia College of Textiles and Sciences and holds a Master's degree from Columbia University. He and his wife Linda have four children, Joshua, Randi, Eric, and Allison.

RICK WOLFF is a well-known baseball writer and commentator. A 1974 graduate of Harvard University, Wolff was drafted and signed by the Detroit Tigers and played two years in the Tigers' chain. Since his professional playing days, Wolff served as the head coach of Mercy College (NY) for seven years, sending several players on to the professional ranks.

Wolff, who holds a Master's degree from Long Island University, has also served as a color commentator for college baseball broadcasts on ESPN and the Madison Square Garden Cable Network, including the 1986 College World Series on ESPN. Wolff and his wife Trish have two children, John and Alyssa.